CURRENT PATTERNS in FIELD INSTRUCTION
in Graduate Social Work Education

Edited by *BETTY LACY JONES*

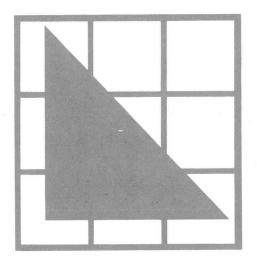

COUNCIL ON SOCIAL WORK EDUCATION
345 East 46th Street   New York, N.Y.   10017

PREFACE

FIELD INSTRUCTION is an integral and indispensable element of the curriculum of a school of social work. In this day of major educational re-examination and restructuring, such an essential part of the curriculum cannot and should not pass unnoticed. The purpose of this new Council publication, *Current Patterns in Field Instruction in Graduate Social Work Education,* is to provide a new look at field instruction and at the changes that have already taken place, that are taking place, and that need to take place.

The articles in this volume—many of them by directors or coordinators of field instruction in schools of social work—are divided into five sections. First covered is an overview of the current state of field instruction with a delineation of its parts that may be combined in various patterns. The other sections, "Settings and Practice Methods," "Teaching and Learning," "Evaluation of Student Performance," and "Administration of Field Instruction," examine different facets of field instruction and current development and new ideas.

Dr. Betty Lacy Jones, CSWE consultant on Field Instruction, served as compiler and editor of the papers in this volume. The Council wishes to extend sincere thanks to her for her efforts and time spent in selecting and editing this valuable collection of articles, and for her work in preparing the introduction to this volume. Grateful acknowledgment is also made to the authors for use of their papers in this collection. The Council expresses its appreciation to the National Institute of Mental Health, Health Services and Mental Health Administration, HEW, for its support of CSWE's work in field instruction and the publication of this volume. A list of other CSWE publications in field instruction will be found on page 176 of this volume.

It is the Council's hope that this volume, as well as other recent CSWE publications in this area, will prove to be of value to directors and teachers of field instruction connected with agencies and schools of social work. In addition, we hope that *Current Patterns in Field Instruction in Graduate Social Work Education* will be of use to all social work educators and agency staff in defining the role of field instruction within the total social work curriculum and in elucidating the connection between agency and school that field instruction can provide.

ARNULF M. PINS
Executive Director

May, 1969

iii

CONTENTS

INTRODUCTION

THE ARTICLES in this volume, *Current Patterns in Field Instruction in Graduate Social Work Education,* were selected from those presented at the CSWE Annual Program Meetings of 1967, 1968, and 1969 and those submitted to the Council for publication or published in its two periodicals[1] during the years of 1967 and 1968. The number of articles from which we had to choose attested to the current active and widespread interest in field instruction. Many pertinent articles of high quality were omitted because of space limitations and because of the intent to cover both selected issues basic to field instruction and a variety of approaches to it.

The Council on Social Work Education has helped to focus attention on the goals and quality of field instruction through a number of its activities. Special impetus was provided by its Project on Field Instruction, which is supported by a grant from the National Institute of Mental Health, Health Services and Mental Health Administration, U.S. Department of Health, Education, and Welfare. Council publications resulting from Project activities include *Field Instruction in Graduate Social Work Education: Old Problems and New Proposals* (1966) and *Field Learning and Teaching: Explorations in Graduate Social Work Education* (1968).

Field instruction, as developed in social work education, is an accomplishment in which the profession can take pride. Other professions such as engineering, medicine, and education are now seeking ways to involve students early in their education in the actual work of their profession.[2] Why, then, this current examination, re-evaluation, tinkering with, and restructuring of field instruction in social work?

Education for social work had its beginnings in the field. The development of supervision as a sophisticated skill took place at the same time that theory, concepts, and a knowledge base were being identified and developed for the new profession.[3] To become a profession, we had

---

[1] *The Journal of Education for Social Work* and the *Social Work Education Reporter.*

[2] Jerrold Zacharias, "Zacharias on Professional Education," *Change in Higher Education,* Vol. 1, No. 1 (January-February, 1969), pp. 30-32.

[3] Bertha Reynolds, *Learning and Teaching in the Practice of Social Work* (New York: Farrar and Rinehart, Inc., 1945); Virginia P. Robinson, *Supervision in Social Casework* (Chapel Hill: University of North Carolina Press, 1936); Charlotte Towle, *The Learner in Education for the Professions* (Chicago: The University of Chicago Press, 1954).

to progress from the particulars of practice in individual agencies to commonalities, to generalizations, to identifying a generic base for professional practice.[4] "The initial stage of formal professional training was concerned with the gaining and organizing of knowledge. . . . But there came a time when knowledge for its own sake became secondary in importance to skill in the use of knowledge."[5] In the nineteen-thirties the impact on social work of psychological theories of personality development refocused attention on class curricula. During the same decade, as an aftermath of the Depression, the development of national governmental welfare structures exercised an opposing force which demanded that attention be given to the practice sector of social work education, particularly the new kinds of practice and practice settings being created.

Another strain in the relationship between class and field teaching developed as differences were identified between supervision of agency staff members and supervision of students. With social work's emergence as a profession, schools of social work began to question the academic quality of that large proportion of their curricula devoted to field work. As Kendall so aptly put it, "all professional education suffers the Janus fate, with one head facing the academic world and the other head facing the workaday world of the profession."[6]

More recent attention by social work educators to theories about the nature of learning suggested that curriculum development emphasize the "structure of subject matter"[7] and reflect the educational principles of continuity, sequence, and integration.[8] Both the importance of organizing principles[9] for effective learning and the proliferation of knowledge and its quick obsolescence made it mandatory that "much emphasis be placed in the schools on the development of generalized ways of attacking problems and on knowledge which can be applied to a

---

[4] Mildred Sikkema, "A Proposal for An Innovation in Field Learning and Teaching," *Field Instruction in Graduate Social Work Education: Old Problems and New Proposals* (New York: Council on Social Work Education, 1966), pp. 1-7.

[5] Kenneth L. M. Pray, "Education for Social Work," *Social Work in a Revolutionary Age* (Philadelphia: University of Pennsylvania Press, 1949), pp. 12-13.

[6] Katherine A. Kendall, "Selected Issues in Field Instruction in Education for Social Work," *Field Instruction—Selected Issues* (New York: Council on Social Work Education, 1959), p. 7.

[7] Jerome S. Bruner, *The Process of Education* (New York: Vintage Books, 1960), pp. 17-32.

[8] *Curriculum Policy Statement* (New York: Council on Social Work Education, 1962), p. 7.

[9] David R. Krathwohl, "The Psychological Bases for Integration," *The Integration of Educational Experiences*, Nelson B. Henry, ed. (Chicago: The National Society for the Study of Education, 1958), pp. 43-65.

wide range of new situations."[10] Such generalization led to higher levels of conceptualization in classroom teaching and, therefore, to problems in establishing connections with the specifics of practice in field instruction.

Out of this dynamic tension between field and class teaching two convictions became crystallized: one, that field work is an indispensable part of the curriculum, and two, that schools of social work must carry primary responsibility for their total curricula—including field instruction. Though in 1951 Hollis and Taylor wrote that "the objectives of field teaching should be identical with those of classroom work and should be as carefully organized into teaching units,"[11] and Boehm, in the 1959 curriculum study, reiterated that field instruction is "an integral part of professional education,"[12] schools continue to seek ways more nearly to achieve these goals. Over the years, curriculum policy statements have consistently affirmed the central importance of field instruction. A current revision in process is no exception, but it has a primary intention of opening the door to variety and change.

There is no doubt that field instruction is changing. There is beginning to be doubt, however, about what field instruction is and there is some question about some of the forms it is taking. Change inevitably brings dislocation, hesitancy, and uncertainty. We need, therefore, to establish some agreement concerning field instruction and a framework that allows for flexible analysis. In 1959, Kendall examined the issues of field instruction—patterns, goals, method, content, and dual responsibility of school and agency—and she asked whether field teaching had more characteristics in common with classroom teaching than with agency practice.[13] In 1965, Schubert posed four major curriculum policy issues in field instruction having to do with the relation between class and field courses and asked: "Should the educational objective in field work be on skill in practice (with repetitive experience in doing) or on knowledge about practice?"[14] Hale, in 1966, listed the characteristics of and stresses on the traditional model of field instruction and stated that "the first parameter which shapes [educational] planning is the set of objectives the educational system seeks to reach."[15] Clearly, the direc-

[10] Benjamin S. Bloom, ed., *Taxonomy of Educational Objectives, Handbook I: Cognitive Domain* (New York: David McKay Co., Inc., 1956), p. 40.

[11] Ernest V. Hollis and Alice L. Taylor, *Social Work Education in the United States* (New York: Columbia University Press, 1951), p. 242.

[12] Werner W. Boehm, *Objectives of the Social Work Curriculum of the Future,* Vol. I of *The Curriculum Study,* Werner W. Boehm, ed. (New York: Council on Social Work Education, 1959), p. 154.

[13] Kendall, *op. cit.,* pp. 1-9.

[14] Margaret S. Schubert, "Curriculum Policy Dilemmas in Field Instruction," *Journal of Education for Social Work,* Vol. 1, No. 2 (Fall, 1965), pp. 38-39.

[15] Mark P. Hale, "The Parameters of Agency-School Social Work Educational Planning," *Journal of Education for Social Work,* Vol. 2, No. 1 (Spring, 1966), p. 33.

tion during the past decade has been to strengthen field instruction as an educational experience.

Present changes in field instruction seem consistent with this emphasis on the educational purpose and content of field instruction. Yet, at the same time that theoretical material is being taught in the field, material from students' own practice is being introduced in the classroom through use of written, taped, and filmed materials. Direct or vicarious experience is also made part of classroom learning through role play, simulation, observation, and experiences with individuals and groups in the immediate community. The dividing line between class and field instruction seems to be blurring. Field instruction is becoming more like classroom instruction and classroom instruction is, in some instances, being moved to the field. Is there an essential difference?

Experiments with location of "the field" began with detaching the student unit from the routine of agency operation and later progressed, in some schools, to moving the field placement out of the agency entirely to a community or campus-based setting. After the establishment of such field or teaching centers, a few schools began to move class instruction to the centers—first the methods classes and then certain other classes. In one school, for example, students take only one course on campus and have all their other classes in the training center. Another pattern is to establish a third location for teaching—the laboratory—where some of the content formerly taught in both class and field is now presented.

It seems that neither "field" nor "instruction" describes a unique function for field instruction, yet there is broad agreement on the need for it. Its essential and unique element, of course, is learning *to do*. In the classroom, wherever it is located, students learn *about*. In the "field," students learn "how to do" through carrying responsibility for delivery of a social service. We also need to make a distinction between practice experience and other learning experiences that can take place in the field or may best occur there. Extra-class experiences can serve many educational purposes, a primary one being the integration of educational experience,[16] but experiences such as serving as clinic escort for underprivileged children or as friendly visitor or observer in a mental hospital, while offering valuable learning experiences in work with people, do not constitute the practice of social work or the delivery of social services. Finally, since most social services are provided under institutional auspices, field instruction requires the participation of social agencies and host institutions. Learning to practice social work can only take place in the field. Locations in which students are gathered to discuss this practice may vary, and learning other than methods of prac-

---

[16] Ruth Churchill and Philip Rothman, "Extraclass Experience," *The Integration of Educational Experience*, Nelson B. Henry, ed. (Chicago: The University of Chicago Press, 1958), pp. 126-142.

tice takes place in the field. Neither the location of discussion nor the other learning should be confused, however, with the essential element of field instruction: the practice activity that tests out and acts to integrate the whole of professional education and from which emerges the beginning professional practitioner.

To recapitulate: in the past and currently the differences between class and field instruction have been examined to their mutual enrichment. Fashioning an integrated whole from two disparate parts has required concentration first on one and then on the other, and this has been difficult. The purpose, methods, and content of field instruction have changed to reflect changing knowledge and social conditions as well as to achieve a unified educational focus. Response to the ferment of change is and should be varied, and there is no consensus on any one pattern for field instruction. There is consensus that practice experience is an imperative component of social work education. "Without practice theory becomes mere speculation. . . . Efforts to connect theory and practice more closely are important contributions to professional education. Social work education has pioneered in this movement."[17] That is why field instruction is necessary and, because we are pioneering, we have the hard job of fashioning new models.[18]

After attempting to answer the question *why* field instruction is needed, we found the following questions[19] about field instruction to be helpful in identifying the parts of field instruction that are arranged in different combinations to form individual patterns in schools of social work.

What is curriculum content for field instruction?
Where does field instruction take place?
Who is the field instructor?[20]
How is the teaching done?
When does field instruction take place and for how long?

---

[17] Ralph W. Tyler, "Distinctive Attributes of Education for the Professions," *A Source Book of Readings on Teaching in Social Work: Reprints of Selected Articles* (New York: Council on Social Work Education, 1965), p. 11.

[18] Hale's article in this volume delineates "traditional" and "innovative" models for field instruction.

[19] Among others who have used this framework effectively is Harriet M. Bartlett in *Analyzing Social Work Practice by Fields* (New York: National Association of Social Workers, 1961).

[20] This question could also relate to students' characteristics and their contribution to field instruction. For student characteristics see Arnulf M. Pins, *Who Chooses Social Work, When and Why?* (New York: Council on Social Work Education, 1963). A publication scheduled for release in winter, 1969, brings the Pins study up to date: *Students in Schools of Social Work: A Study of Characteristics and Factors Affecting Career Choice and Practice Concentration* by Deborah Golden, Arnulf Pins, and Wyatt C. Jones.

The topics under which the articles in this collection are grouped were determined by these questions. Some articles cover several issues but have been grouped according to their primary focus. In the following discussion of the five questions, both primary and secondary foci are indicated in order to facilitate their location in the collection.

The first question in the series of five questions—*what?*—has to do with educational objectives and the content of field instruction. Schubert, in her article in the section entitled "Overview," says that two main approaches to educational objectives seem possible: a problem approach and a methods approach. The latter approach receives some attention in Borsuk's description of the University of Louisville's first-year field instruction plan and in Abels's article based on Case Western Reserve's field instruction in community organization, but little attention is given it in other articles.[21]

Variations in methods concentrations are amply illustrated in this volume. A few articles are primarily concerned with concentration on one or another of the primary methods, for example, Abels's with group work and Rothman's with community organization. Meyer, Rose *et al.*, and Werner discuss programs in which two or more discrete methods are taught, usually casework combined with group work and/or elements of community organization. There is interest in breadth in methods teaching, but Baker underscores the concomitant need to continue educating the casework clinician. The teaching of integrated methods is illustrated in various contexts in the articles by Borsuk, Cassidy, Di-Paola, Kelley *et al.*, Selyan, and Schutz.

Curriculum content must be determined by and reflect the goals and purposes both of social work as a whole and of the individual school; McGuire, for one, makes this point. The ordering of field work curricula and the selection of practice experiences and knowledge content are touched on in most of the articles, especially in Rothman's, and receive particular emphasis in the articles in the third section, "Teaching and Learning."

Once educational goals and curriculum content are determined, schools can devise a variety of solutions to the last four questions: *where* does field instruction take place, *who* teaches it, *how* is it taught, and *when* and for how long is field instruction offered? These solutions are also affected by the availability of resources and talents, by faculty and student interests, by location of the school, and by its adherence to particular theories of learning and instruction. In other words, the answers to the four questions are determined partly by the particular educational approach, partly by specific educational goals and curricu-

---

[21] A recent article concerned with post-master's education illustrates the problem approach. See Lydia Rapoport and Robert Z. Apte, "Advanced Education for Practice in Community Mental Health," *Social Work Education Reporter*, Vol. 16, No. 4 (December, 1968), pp. 24ff.

lum design, partly by exigencies and practical considerations, partly by individual preferences, and, perhaps, partly by chance.

The second question—*where?*—refers to the location of field instruction. We have already seen that locations for field instruction can be most varied, and that the determinants of any given variation include the goal and curriculum for field instruction. In considering the location of field instruction, there are several factors which characterize a setting. It may be located in a social agency, in a host organization, in an independent setting, or on campus. The settings in which field instruction takes place may be administered by a social agency, a host organization, or the school of social work. The students' practice may take place in one or several social agencies or other kinds of organizations. A school-administered program may be located in either a host agency or in the school's own facility. In the school's facility, other social service agencies or departments may participate in staffing and program determination. The factors of administration of field instruction setting, practice setting, and social service program are combined in various ways to produce six different types of settings for field instruction which are illustrated in this volume.

Agency Placements

1. The single agency placement is the most familiar. Field instruction setting, practice setting, and social service program are all administered by one agency. If the agency offers several services, it is possible for the student's experience to have breadth as well as depth. Meyer, though writing about a school-administered service, illustrates the breadth of practice experience available in a hospital setting. Glover, in an editorial in *Child Welfare*, pointed out the breadth and diversity of practice experience available in child welfare agencies.[22] DiPaola's and Schubert's articles point to the opportunities for both breadth and specialization in methods of practice in the traditional agency placement.

2. Practice experience in agency placements may also be diversified by subsidiary or satellite practice experiences in social services outside the agency that serves as setting for field instruction and provides the primary practice experience.

Teaching Centers

3. A teaching center may be established in a social agency but operate more or less independently of the agency, although the agency may provide some of the students' practice experience. The administration of the setting is the responsibility of the agency; both agency and school share the administration of practice, and other agencies provide settings for brief practice experiences.

---

[22] E. Elizabeth Glover, "The Foster Care Agency: A Unique Resource for Social Work Education," Editor's Page, *Child Welfare*, Vol. 46, No. 2 (February, 1967), pp. 64 and 103.

4. Closely related to this type of teaching center is the center situated in an independent location. Practice experience is provided through the cooperation of a number of agencies. The latter agencies may include established social services or host agencies in which the students develop social services for the people served in other ways by the host organization. Cassidy's article illustrates both of these patterns; Borsuk's illustrates the latter.

5. Another variation of administrative responsibility is found in the teaching center that is located in a host institution in which the school contracts to provide social services to the clientele of the host institution. Meyer describes a school-administered social service department in a hospital.

Service Centers

6. The final main type of field setting is the service center, administered by the school to provide both education and social services. Brieland describes the ways in which established agencies cooperate in providing staff and determining services in the school-administered center.

So far in our analytical framework we have raised the questions *what* and *where*. The third question asks *who* are the field instructors. Here we are concerned primarily with their preparation and with whether they are school or agency employees or whether they are full-time or part-time field instructors. Full-time field faculty are still in the minority; in 1968 there were 961 full-time field instructors, 731 of whom were school employees as compared to 3,372 part-time field instructors, 93 of whom were employed by schools.[23]

It is significant that the authors who describe innovations in teaching methods sequences or innovations in settings speak to the importance of school-employed or full-time field instructors to carrying out their programs. Cassidy, for example, makes very clear the significance of the faculty-employed field instructor in the accomplishment of specified educational goals. DiPaola's article, however, describes the careful process of "retooling" required of field instructors, the majority of whom are agency employees. Persons with the most skill, knowledge, and experience may be available for field instruction in either school or agency, depending on time and locality. Length of tenure of field instructor may also be adversely or positively affected by either school or agency policies. Certainly, integration of class and field learning is simplified and innovations are facilitated when field instructors are school employees and have job responsibilities that bring them fre-

---

[23] *Statistics on Social Work Education, 1968* (New York: Council on Social Work Education, 1969), p. 42. Also see Richard Onken, *A Survey of Faculty in Graduate Schools of Social Work* (New York: Council on Social Work Education, 1968).

quently to campus and in contact with classroom faculty. Conversely, intimate knowledge of and direct involvement in agency structure and awareness of innovations in practice and of changing client needs usually can be brought more readily to field instruction by agency supervisors than by school-employed field instructors.

Werner, Cassidy, and DiPaola all make very clear the role of field instructors as educators, the demand on them for a broad knowledge of social work methodology and of changes in and additions to classroom curricula, and the need for schools to provide assistance to field instructors in maintaining a certain standard of scholarship.

The fourth question is related to teaching methodology: *how* is field instruction taught? The third section of this volume is devoted to discussion of this question and of ways to integrate class and practice learning.

Finestone's article provides a bridge from the consideration of patterns and settings for field instruction to a focus on methods of teaching and theories of learning in field instruction. In two companion articles, Selyan examines these within the pattern of block field placements and Schutz considers them in the context of the concurrent field-class plan. The three kinds of learning delineated by Walter Kindelsperger—cognitive, vicarious, and practice experience[24]—are illustrated by Rothman's article. The classroom is seen as the primary site for cognitive learning, the field as the primary site for practice experience. The intermediate type of learning—making use of old and new media, audiotapes, videotapes, case records, and of simulation, role playing, and group discussion focused on practice, social problems, or social systems—may take place in the classroom, in the field, or in a laboratory or seminar.[25] A topic related to the "how" of field instruction that does not receive attention in this volume is the use of group and individual teaching. The merits of both have been demonstrated. A planned combination of these methods takes advantage of the strengths of each.

The two articles on evaluation of student performance deal with another aspect of teaching, that of measuring the results of education

---

[24] Walter L. Kindelsperger, "Modes of Adult Learning in Preparation for the Service Professions," *Field Learning and Teaching: Explorations in Graduate Social Work Education* (New York: Council on Social Work Education, 1967), pp. 33-36.

[25] See, for example: Morton S. Perlmutter and Gary Gumpert, "Field Instruction and Group Process: An Experiment in the Use of Television," *Social Work Education Reporter*, Vol. 15, No. 3 (September, 1967), pp. 26-29; Marguerite V. Pohek, "Report on Developments in Teaching and Teaching Methodology," *Social Work Education Reporter*, Vol. 16, No. 2 (June, 1968), pp. 20-21; Sanford N. Sherman, "Teaching Casework Through Participant Observation," *Social Casework*, Vol. 44, No. 10 (December, 1968), pp. 595-601; and Lila Swell, "Role-Playing in the Context of Learning Theory in Casework Teaching," *Journal of Education for Social Work*, Vol. 4, No. 1 (Spring, 1968), pp. 70-76.

against educational goals. The first article deals with evaluation of multi-methods practice and the second with casework and group work. It should be noted that there were far fewer articles concerned with research than with any other aspect of field instruction.[26]

The final question that formed our framework for considering field instruction had to do with *when:* with timing, the point at which field instruction is offered, and its duration. The two articles dealing most directly with one aspect of this question are those by Selyan and Schutz, which present, in that order, rationales for block field instruction and for concurrent field and classroom instruction. No article deals directly with the amount of time that should be spent in field instruction. Attention, peripheral to the focus of other articles, is given to delayed entry to field instruction, orientation,[27] timing of assignment of service responsibility, and various arrangements of concurrent field work time.

In summary, educationally directed practice experience is the unique contribution of field instruction. The emerging variety in patterns of field instruction gives promise for increasing both the quality of social work education and the number of students who can be accommodated within existing and developing resources. Our profession must recognize and continue to employ field instruction patterns of proven usefulness. It must combine these with new knowledge and methods. Our thanks are extended to the authors in this volume whose sense of social work's past, present, and future so ably informs the articles presented in the five sections that follow: An Overview of Field Instruction, Settings and Practice Methods, Teaching and Learning in the Field, Evaluation of Student Performance, and Administration of Field Instruction.

---

[26] An outstanding example of research in field instruction is: Margaret Schubert, *Field Instruction in Social Casework: A Report of an Experiment* (Chicago: Social Service Monographs, Second Series, The School of Social Service Administration, The University of Chicago, 1963).

[27] For a recent article on orientation, see Merle M. Foeckler, "Orientation to Field Instruction in Light of Current Needs of Social Work Education," *Social Work Education Reporter*, Vol. 16, No. 3 (September, 1968), pp. 34-35 and 45-46.

PART I
AN OVERVIEW OF
FIELD INSTRUCTION

MAKING THE BEST USE OF TRADITIONAL AND ATYPICAL FIELD PLACEMENTS

MARGARET SCHUBERT

How can one give breadth of learning experience in a field placement that involves perhaps only one student with one field instructor in one agency with a limited range of services? How can one give depth—a chance to master some aspect of social work practice—in a multi-service agency or in a teaching situation that is outside agency structure? These questions are uppermost as one considers ways of utilizing to the maximum traditional and atypical field placements.

During recent years, there has been an extraordinary preoccupation with the form and structure of field work. Questions about form and structure have to do with such elements as the following:

1. Under what auspices should the service to clients be given? Should it be under the auspices of an established agency or should it be under the auspices of the school in a specially designed teaching situation?
2. Under what auspices should the teaching take place? Should the instruction be given by persons who are employed by agencies or by persons employed by the school? To what extent should the school in either case have control of the educational content?
3. What arrangements of time are desirable? Should there be block placements for one year or both years of the graduate program? Should the assignment be continuous for a period of 12 to 15 months? Should there be an arbitrary decision about concurrent field work for two days a week in the first year and three in the

MARGARET SCHUBERT is a professor at the Richmond School of Social Work of Virginia Commonwealth University. This paper was originally presented at the Council on Social Work Education Seventeenth Annual Program Meeting in Cleveland, Ohio, January, 1969.

second, or two in both years, or three in both years? Should there be a gradual introduction with perhaps one day of field work to begin with and as much as four or five days toward the end of the educational experience? Or should the amount of time devoted to field work be arranged with complete flexibility according to individual student needs?

4. How many placements should a student experience in the course of the graduate program? One during the entire master's degree period, one for each year, or more?
5. How many students should be assigned to one instructor? A single student, a unit of four, five, six, or even 12? Should several units be joined together under the tutelage of a group of teachers?
6. Should field instruction be arranged so that the teaching is done mainly or entirely through individual conferences, exclusively through group conferences, or through some arbitrary or more flexible combination of individual and group conferences?[1]

Some of this preoccupation with form and structure seems to be a reaction against apprenticeship. The word "apprenticeship" is, at present, in disrepute. I have contributed to this depreciation of apprenticeship by stating elsewhere that it implies a fixed way of doing things in a situation which is viewed as static rather than as rapidly changing. It is interesting to note that, at the same time that the word "apprenticeship" has gained such ill repute in the master's program, it has been seriously suggested—in connection with one doctoral program—that a very good way for a student to learn how to be a researcher is to apprentice himself to an experienced researcher who is involved in a vital area of subject matter. Certainly apprenticeship, if it involves an intimate contact with a curious and wide-ranging mind, should have many positives about it; there is no need to depreciate this form of learning when such contact is involved. In general, however, the effort to get away from apprenticeship in its less savory aspects involves a commitment to identifiable educational goals, with specification of curriculum content and desired outcomes.

A particular structure may be simply a response to certain exigencies. Limited agency resources in the neighborhood of the school may dictate block placements distant from the school; a school-employed field instructor may be essential when the agency is unable to provide an instructor; perhaps a school, when developing something new in an area of practice which is not yet common in the agencies, may find it necessary to give much more active leadership through a school-employed instructor; at times agency instructors may be used because the

---

[1] For elaboration on some of these questions, see *Field Learning and Teaching* (New Orleans: Tulane University School of Social Work, 1968), or *Field Learning and Teaching: Explorations in Graduate Social Work Education* (New York: Council on Social Work Education, 1967).

school cannot afford to employ instructors, and at times because the agency instructor has a higher degree of competence. While I recognize the practical problems that may be a determining factor here, I would like to limit this paper to the relationship of structure to educational objectives.

It is possible to imagine educational objectives that focus entirely on social planning or on independent practice outside current organizations. I assume for the moment, however, that most schools are still concerned with educating students who are able to perform some service within existing agencies, even though there may be considerable focus on learning ways of altering established agencies and improving their methods of service.[2] Given such objectives, two main approaches seem possible. First, a problem approach[3] and second, a methods approach. Within the problem approach, one might seek to help the student acquire mastery of a particular human problem area. This implies command of relevant knowledge about, say, the aging. It implies also an ability to select and use any social work method that is relevant or to select the appropriate method and achieve mastery of one method related to this problem area. Another possible objective within the problem approach would be to help the student gain mastery of methods of problem area analysis: command of knowledge about how to get the relevant knowledge.

Given a methods approach to objectives, one could conceive of a number of variations. One might seek mastery of one method and ability to use it in one type of agency or in a variety of settings. Or there might be concentration in one method with some ability to use others in one type of agency or in a variety of settings. And, finally, one might envision an objective that includes the use of multiple methods in one type of agency or in a variety.

In deciding on the educational objectives in the field, several criteria need to be kept in mind:

1. The needs of the field now and in the future.
2. The interests of students.
3. The feasibility of the students achieving the objectives within the educational period allowed.
4. The transferability of learning to situations beyond those encountered during the educational program.
5. The present and potential availability of learning experiences that will support the objectives.

---

[2] Problems that arise when school and agency take disparate views are discussed by Carol H. Meyer and Mary R. Baker in "Integrating Practice Demands in Social Work Education," *Social Casework*, Vol. 49, No. 8 (October, 1968), pp. 481-488.

[3] Henry S. Maas, "Social Work Knowledge and Social Responsibility," *Journal of Education for Social Work*, Vol. 4, No. 1, (Spring, 1968), pp. 37-48.

Decisions related to the first four criteria usually have to be made on the basis of incomplete information. We know that even now existing institutions need social work staff who have special competence in particular problem areas and special competence in particular methods. The form which these institutions may take in the future is by no means clear and we are forced to make some assumptions that skills learned in one situation may be applicable in a changed situation. We also know that the interests of the students who are just entering graduate education may change before the end of the master's program, and that career patterns are by no means permanently fixed. Since one's perceptions are in large part guided by or even determined by one's knowledge and theoretical orientation, educators are properly concerned that a student's educational experience should be broad enough that he will not graduate with what has been called "trained incompetence." If education is too narrow, then the tendency to do what one is competent to do may well result in an inappropriate application of a method. Our impulse toward offering breadth of educational experiences is again modified by our concern that the objectives be realistic of accomplishment. The question always arises as to how much a student can encompass in the limited period of time available, a question which has not yet been answered by experience. Perhaps more evidence will be available after some of the multi-method and problem-focused field programs have been in action for a longer period. In the meantime, some educators are operating on the conviction that a wide range of knowledge and skill can be attained in two years and others are operating on the conviction that relative mastery of one method is the most that can be expected.

Whatever choice is made as to objectives, it is essential that they be clearly stated in terms of the kinds of behavior expected of the student at the end of the master's program, and it is necessary to assess the availability of learning experiences that will support the objectives. The student should have a chance in the course of his education to practice the behavior that is desired as an end product. It is the opportunity for practice that determines whether modification in structure of the course is necessary. If mastery of a problem area is desired, with mastery of the relevant knowledge and an ability to use all social work methods in relation to one problem area, it seems fairly clear that no one existing agency and no one instructor could provide all the opportunities that are required. Practice experience bounded within one agency or even within two would be most unlikely to offer the range of experiences that is desirable. If the objective is skill in all social work methods, it also seems quite clear that few existing agencies will offer equal opportunity for the full range of practice.

Whatever the objectives may be, the qualifications of the teacher are of central importance in making possible their achievement. I submit that the looser the structure of the field course and the wider the range

6

of possible learning experiences, the more expertness is required of the teacher. Full knowledge of a problem area such as retardation or aging, full knowledge of all the services available, and full knowledge of helping methods that range from individual counseling to large-scale national program planning, are unlikely to be vested in one person. Even when these difficulties are overcome by team teaching, someone must select and arrange the experiences to which the student is to be exposed and someone must assist the student in analyzing and evaluating those experiences. Anyone who has tried knows that it is infinitely more time-consuming to plan an observation and help the student in his analysis of the observation than it is to assign responsibility for a case. Team teaching is expensive in terms of personnel. Any teaching that goes beyond the assignment and supervision of a particular task requires an increased investment by the instructor. When a school tries to make sure that all its students will have field learning experiences that go beyond the encounter with the individual client, the school's investment in preparing field instructors to carry out this task is increased, particularly when there is a large turnover in instructors. Many of the costs of field instruction are hidden or ignored, and, so far as I know, there has never been a thorough study of the relative cost of the various teaching plans now in operation. Perhaps such a study has never been undertaken simply because the findings would be too frightening, but I believe that sooner or later it is incumbent upon us to assess the extent to which we achieve our stated objectives by various forms of teaching and to give an accurate accounting of their costs.

The 1962 *Curriculum Policy Statement* of the Council on Social Work Education has been one of the forces pushing us toward enlargement of the objectives of field teaching, and some of the rearrangements of the field course have been undertaken in the expectation that modifications of structure would help to implement attainment of the objectives. I shall not review here the many experiments now underway or contemplated but refer you rather to Mildred Sikkema's report.[4] She lists four atypical placement structures in addition to what is referred to as the traditional agency concept. They are as follows:

1. The *Traditional Agency Concept* in each of the two years with some form of educational control of quality in teaching, curriculum design, objectives, content, and learning opportunities.
2. *The Teaching Center Concept* in one or both years with educational control of quality in school-employed field teachers, curriculum design, objectives, content, and learning opportunities.
3. *The Service Center Concept* in which teaching-learning, demonstration, and research functions (the latter function in one such center) are coordinate functions with services to a community. The teaching-

---

[4] *Field Learning and Teaching,* Tulane, 1968, and *Field Learning and Teaching,* CSWE, 1967, *ibid.*

learning function (and research in one such center) is under school control, with educational control of quality as in (2) above.

4. *A Social Problem Area Concept* as a second-year model with a one-agency placement, but with some utilization of agencies in the "organized group of selected agencies called a teaching-learning complex in the social problem area" with educational control of quality as in (2) and (3) above.

5. *A Social Problem Area Concept* as a first-year, school-based model with educational control of quality as in (2), (3), and (4) above.[5]

Several pieces of research on the evaluation of field work outcomes during the last ten years indicate that a considerable variation of structure can be undertaken without disadvantage to the student. Some of the faculties who are engaged in distinctly new patterns of instruction have the strong impression that students are benefited by such experience but, as yet, we do not have any very hard evidence about the ways in which the benefit is demonstrated or the relative values of different types of structure. For those who are concerned about "depth" in the atypical settings, there is comfort in noting that so far field instruction has been carried out by a teaching staff who are themselves competent in some area of practice and therefore almost inevitably tend to offer the student a concentration in that area in which the instructor has special knowledge. Whether or not the move toward teaching students in the field in groups will have the desired effect of helping the graduate move more rapidly toward responsible independent practice is still unknown.

It is probably safe to say that, at the present time, no school wants to offer its students a narrow field experience that is little more than in-service training, and that few schools, if any, are in a position to undertake a restructuring of the field course that would involve vastly increased costs. Let us then consider ways in which a fairly traditional field setting can be used to broaden a student's knowledge and increase the range of his skill so that he will be better fitted to move into the changing field of professional practice. This focus seems appropriate in view of the large number of students, perhaps half of all master's degree students, who are placed with agency field instructors, each of whom has responsibility for teaching one or two students at a time. (This estimate is based on the 1966 figures from CSWE which showed approximately 9,500 MSW students in field work with over 4,000 field instructors, more than 3,000 of whom were part-time and paid by the agency.[6])

An essential task in designing a series of learning experiences in a given setting is to make an inventory of the experiences available and the levels of responsibility which it is possible for a student to assume. By level of responsibility, I mean a continuum such as the following:

---

[5] *Ibid.*, pp. 19-20.
[6] CSWE reference.

1. Hearing or reading about a process
2. Observing a process
3. Participating in a process
4. Carrying professional responsibility

An inventory of available experiences might employ such items as these:

1. The social work methods employed
   a. Casework (including joint interviews and family treatment)
   b. Group work
   c. Collaborative work with other disciplines and other agencies related to either casework or group work services
   d. Community organization
   e. Administration
   f. Research
2. The span of time available for the service
3. The phases of the process
   a. Initial phase (such as intake in casework or problem formulation in research)
   b. The continued work in the process
   c. Termination or conclusion
4. The types of problems with which the agency offers help
5. The social characteristics of the persons who use agency services
   a. Age
   b. Race
   c. Sex
   d. Marital Status
   e. Financial Resources
   f. Educational background

Most agencies have far more learning experiences available than they recognize. The student may not be able to carry professional responsibility in every one of the methods or in all phases of a process in each method, and possibly he may not be able to participate in all of them, but, as a minimum, he could observe many of them and at least hear and read about others. Every agency, regardless of its particular helping services, is somehow involved with the community and with other agencies. Every agency has an administrative process of some kind and it is hard to imagine an agency that does not have unsolved problems which pose researchable questions. The extent to which the field instructor can make use of all possible experiences depends in part upon the accuracy of his inventory of potential experiences but even more upon his knowledge of relevant concepts. By concepts, I mean the terms in which a particular experience can be analyzed so that learning can be applied in new situations.

The casework teacher in what we are calling the "traditional" field placement already has at his command a number of conceptual tools. He has names for the intake process and the purposes of intake and initial interviews. He can help a student to analyze and compare marital conflict in young couples and older people or to compare the problems in placing a child and in hospitalizing an older person with terminal illness. The quality of his teaching will be enhanced as he makes these concepts explicit and helps the student to apply them from one situation to the next and even speculate beyond the direct experience he may have in the agency.

Not all instructors, however, are equally at home with the concepts of organization and administration. It is logical that schools should take more responsibility in relation to these somewhat foreign concepts than they have in relation to those with which it is assumed the instructor is already familiar. Reports of different schools' efforts in this direction are beginning to appear in the literature and there is probably a great deal more unpublished material in the hands of individual schools. I quote, for example, the recent article by Merle M. Foeckler, who reports on what is called the "agency-community assignment" at the University of Georgia.

"A basic assumption upon which the entire assignments proceed is that social services are offered in the context of a community (a dynamic ecological entity) . . ." Community is used here in the sense of a "social system occupying a specified (geographical) location. As a system, any change in one element or dimension of the community will result in relatively immediate changes, or adjustments, in every other element or dimension. The form of any given service is crucially shaped by the amount of resources available for allocation for social welfare purposes in the community (economic dimensions); the willingness to allocate these resources to 'recognized' needs in the community (normative dimension); and the process by which rival claims to the allocation of resources are adjudicated (political dimension)."[7]

An example of the unpublished documents is the work currently being done at the Richmond School of Social Work of the Virginia Commonwealth University in an effort to clarify the kinds of observations about policy formation that students may make in field work. A few items in a long and still-tentative list are reproduced below.

Policy evolves and is affected by many forces: staff (at all levels), the executive, the board, the client.

Practice may or may not reflect agency policy; conflicts may exist between explicit policy and the "unwritten policy" of the agency.

Policies tend to become institutionalized and may therefore be hard to change.

---

[7] Merle M. Foeckler, "Orientation to Field Instruction in Light of Current Needs of Social Work Education," *Social Work Education Reporter*, Vol. 16, No. 3 (September, 1968), pp. 34ff.

What is suggested in these brief examples is that most agencies probably have a wider variety of educational experiences available for students than they fully realize, and existing placements could be enriched and broadened by exploiting the resources already present. Simply to bathe in experience is not enough. In so-called traditional settings, the requirement of process recording of client interviews (misused as this requirement may sometimes be) is a step toward analysis of the casework process; it at least guarantees that the student will give thoughtful attention to this interaction. When experience is broadened through a wider range of observations or tasks, it is essential that the student engage in an equally thoughtful analysis. The strength of the agency as a teaching placement lies not merely in the experience available but in the conceptual tools of the teacher who can help the student make maximum use of the experience.

Whether the placement is atypical or traditional, the teacher has a central role in identifying and arranging the learning experiences, in helping the student in the analysis of these experiences, and in evaluating with him the extent to which specified educational goals have been achieved.

FORECASTING THE FUTURE OF FIELD LEARNING AND TEACHING

RITA A. McGUIRE

"IT IS CURIOUSLY difficult to recapture pre-conceptual innocence"[1] state the authors of a significant contribution to the understanding of cognition and cognitive processes in an analysis of the process of concept attainment. For one who has for the past few months been studying the responses to a questionnaire on modifications in field learning and teaching, it is not only difficult but patently foolish to try to recreate that stage of field work development that our present sophistication may now designate as pre-conceptual. Despite a degree of discomfort with language that one supposes serves the useful purpose of a reminder of a not inglorious past—in Mildred Sikkema's words, retaining "the values of apprenticeship learning"[2]—most of the 33 schools responding to the questionnaire reported some work on development of a conceptual framework for the field course. The range was considerable, from modest efforts to consider the major concepts to be taught and learned in field practice, to carefully enunciated categorizations showing the effects of many faculty-field institutes and workshops and committee meetings, and of participation with other schools in Council-sponsored

---

[1] Jerome S. Bruner, Jacqueline J. Goodnow, George A. Austin, A *Study of Thinking* (New York: Science Editions, Inc., 1962), p. 50.
[2] Mildred Sikkema, "A Proposal for an Innovation in Field Learning and Teaching," *Field Instruction in Graduate Social Work Education: Old Problems and New Proposals* (New York: Council on Social Work Education, 1966), p. 7.

RITA A. McGUIRE is associate dean at the School of Social Service, Fordham University. This paper contains highlights of a paper presented at the Sixteenth Annual Program Meeting of the Council on Social Work Education in Minneapolis, Minnesota, January, 1968.

projects. Clearly, the schools reporting and, one can believe, others not reporting for whatever reasons,[3] are well past conceptual ignorance and are moving ahead into a post-conceptual phase, a McLuhan-like understanding of environment that transcends classification of data and brings "integrated tasks, integrated knowledge, and pattern recognition."[4]

To forecast the future of field learning and teaching one must first study the evidence of the present and interpret it in the context of forces influencing social work and social work education, selecting those which seem to have meaning. This paper was viewed at first as an attempt to obtain an overview of current modifications in field practice in order to report on recent innovations and by exchange of information to provide stimulation and challenge. From the comments of faculty supplying data, there could be no question as to the interest of schools in the simple usefulness of exchange, but higher expectations of the data processor in a computer-conscious age suggested prediction of innovations likely to survive. Yet, since the problems of persons are known to be at least as serious as those of machines, the predictions may be less than accurate.

Interest in experimentation and innovation in field instruction has been accelerated by the Council on Social Work Education through a variety of activities. An early endeavor was the work of three schools in undertaking an exploration of (1) whether social work education could use in field instruction a method of curriculum construction similar to that developed for classroom teaching, and (2) what learning opportunities field instructors were using to help students attain objectives other than those directly related to a social work method of concentration. A recent activity, following a number of other projects, was the Symposium of October, 1967, in which 13 schools participated.[5] CSWE

---

[3] Since this was not an official request to schools by CSWE but merely an invitation to participate in a study, the schools had to choose between this and innumerable other demands.

[4] Herbert Marshall McLuhan, "Address at Vision 65," *The American Scholar*, Vol. 35, No. 2 (Spring, 1966), pp. 196-205.

[5] Jeanette Regensburg, "Report of Exploratory Project in Field Instruction," in *Field Instruction in Graduate Social Work Education: Old Problems and New Proposals* (New York: Council on Social Work Education, 1966), pp. 23-56. See also *Field Learning and Teaching: Explorations in Graduate Social Work Education* (New York: Council on Social Work Education, 1968 [not available at time this paper was prepared]). For earlier reports on research in field work see: Margaret Schubert, "Field Work Performance: Achievement Levels of First-Year Students in Selected Aspects of Casework Service," *Social Service Review*, Vol. 32 (June, 1958), pp. 20-37; Mary Lewis, Dorothy Howerton, and Walter Kindelsperger, "An Experimental Design for First-Year Field Instruction" (New Orleans: Tulane University School of Social Work, 1962); Margaret Schubert, *Field Instruction in Social Casework*, (Chicago: Social Service Monographs, Second Series, The School of Social Service Administration, The University of Chicago, 1963).

For research in methods of field instruction, see Rita A. McGuire, "The

Annual Program Meetings have provided an opportunity for schools to report ongoing work on structure, content, and methods in field work.[6] The Community Organization Curriculum Development Project has directed attention to changes in the established field instruction model in community organization.[7] In preparation for the present report, a letter was sent to the deans of the 72 accredited schools of social work (1967 CSWE listing)[8] asking their help in obtaining data on recent modifications in field learning and teaching. It was stated that any alteration in plan or procedure in the past two years would be of interest but that the school's perception of what changes needed to be made and the basis for change, from an educational stance, were the prime considerations. A schedule covering eight aspects or elements in field work was sent with the letter. These eight items seemed, to the writer, to hold the key to development of new models. In order, they are:

1. Formulation of learning objectives for field instruction.
2. Development of a conceptual framework for field curriculum.
3. Application of principles of curriculum construction to field learning and teaching.
4. Learning opportunities and assignments.

Group Work Field Instructor-in-Action," Columbia University, doctoral dissertation, 1963; and Reva Fine Holtzman, "Major Teaching Methods in Field Instruction in Casework," Columbia University, doctoral dissertation, 1966.

For field work in historical perspective, see Mildred Sikkema, "The Objectives of Field Work in Social Casework, 1898-1955," University of Chicago, doctoral dissertation, 1964.

[6] Margaret L. Schutz, "Report of the Field Instruction Experimental Project of the George Warren Brown School of Social Work," and Winifred E. Smith, "The Statement of a Model for Field Instruction Developed at the University of California, Los Angeles, School of Social Welfare"—two papers presented at a Workshop on Experimentation in the Structure, Content, and Arrangements of Field Instruction, Council on Social Work Education, Fourteenth Annual Program Meeting, New York, 1966. An analysis of curriculum innovations reported by schools of social work in 1965 was also presented at the 1966 Annual Program Meeting by Beulah Rothman, "Curriculum Innovations in Social Work Education."

[7] Wyatt C. Jones, assisted by Jack Rothman, "Community Organization Field Instruction: Report of an Informal Survey" (New York: Council on Social Work Education, November, 1966), mimeo; Jack Rothman, "Working Paper on Field Instruction in Community Organization" (New York: Council on Social Work Education, November, 1966), mimeo. Another assessment of the traditional model is offered by Vera Foote in a paper presented at a field instructors' institute at Adelphi University, December 15, 1966, "A Review of the Traditional Model of Field Instruction and a View of Two Innovative Models," mimeo. The innovative models are those at the University of California, Los Angeles, and San Diego State College School of Social Work.

[8] *Graduate Professional Schools of Social Work in Canada and the U.S.A., 1967* (New York: Council on Social Work Education, 1967).

5. Teaching methods and materials.
6. Faculty advising—with students, with field instructors.
7. Efforts to achieve integration of class and field.
8. Educational programs for agency-based field instructors and agency administrators.

In addition to responding to the eight categories, each school was requested to comment briefly on its philosophy regarding the purpose of field instruction, to note any evaluation that had been made, to identify major problems in modifying existing patterns, and to indicate modifications projected for 1967-68. This constituted a large order for a busy dean or field coordinator. That 39 schools answered and 33 of these submitted responses to the schedule and, in some instances, sent materials describing in greater detail current or proposed plans, can be interpreted as evidence of more than casual interest in the problems and issues in field instruction. For schools already committed to major alterations, the questionnaire must have seemed a presumptuous intrusion, but they either had the grace to make no response or to answer fully and candidly. Only one school involved in basic modification stated that it would not be feasible to answer the questionnaire. The generous response of the participating schools is tribute to their interest and concern about field instruction, and their desire to share experiences toward the goal of strengthening field work and developing a more flexible instrument for educating social work students. There was no follow-up on non-respondents, and no claim can be made to a representative survey; there was a substantial range in size and in geographic locations of the schools.

LEARNING OBJECTIVES

Almost all the schools reported work on the formulation of learning objectives, describing "broad objectives" and an attention to a variety of learning patterns. Breadth included teaching integrated methods of practice, orientation to community, and social problems and social systems foci. There was obvious intent "to recast objectives in the perspective of present demands and future expectations of practice."

From a study of the responses regarding educational objectives, it is obvious that schools are more conscious of objectives and that considerable faculty effort is put into their delineation. It seemed difficult for schools to break away from the familiar phraseology of statements that have been prepared over the years. Only when a school makes a serious creative attempt to relate the form and structure of field instruction to its own educational objectives, to emerging social needs, and to new knowledge does it appear that new models can emerge. This seems to have been the experience at the schools trying out a teaching center, or an "agency-community assignment," or regrouping of students into a "community unit" composed of sections of 12 with a field instructor.

CONCEPTUAL FRAMEWORK

Because of the interrelatedness of the first two categories—formulation of learning objectives and development of a conceptual framework —not every school responded in the second category. Responses were also at different levels of abstraction. The following is a typical listing of concepts to be taught in the field:

1. Professional identification and responsibility
2. Functions of values and knowledge in practice
3. Methods, principles, and techniques useful in problem solving
4. Professional relationships
5. Individual, family, group, community, complex organization
6. Social agency structure, function, program, and procedures
7. Observation, interviews, recording, collaborative work
8. Fact finding, psychosocial diagnosis, selection of goals and priorities, problem-solving work
9. Intake, continuing work, referral, collaboral and cooperative work
10. Evaluation

One school questioned how much conceptual content should be in the field, pointing out the need to maintain the balance between "feeling" and "doing."

The impression one has after reflecting on these and other comments about a conceptual framework is that the selection of relevant concepts is possibly the hardest task a faculty is called upon to perform, and that a great deal of preparatory work of classifying may need to be done. As with educational objectives, it is necessary to put aside—temporarily, at least—the old familiar listing and start work on new formations and constellations of ideas. It would be both salutary and practical for social work educators to consider the innovative process itself. Here the analysis of innovations in group work field instruction made by Somers and Gitlin might be broadened to include the entire range of field practice. Among the conclusions reached by these educators is that innovation is the product of a "complex introduction of intellectual climate, chance, social problems and change, practice demands and fertile agency systems, and educated, imaginative thinkers."[9]

---

[9] Mary Louise Somers and Paul Gitlin, "Innovations in Field Instruction in Social Group Work," *Journal of Education for Social Work*, Vol. 2, No. 1 (Spring, 1966), pp. 52-58.

LEARNING OPPORTUNITIES

Almost all the schools expressed the belief that they had developed broader experiences and generally, in illustration, cited work with groups and community. There were descriptions of school-administered centers "for neighborhood development" and "for experimentation in social work practice," in which field work practice and research would both be pursued. Other schools established training centers in neighborhoods and in housing projects in order to provide students with a variety of experience, sometimes in one or more of the discrete methods, sometimes in integrated social work practice. Experience with the enabling methods of social work—supervision, administration, consultation—were also facilitated by center or unit field placements.

INTEGRATION OF CLASS AND FIELD

A fairer question to the schools might have been to ask for their view of integrating class and field, for not all interpret "integration" the same way. The extremes of this continuum included a school that asserted that "integration" is the most perplexing problem and that there is no intent to achieve a one-to-one congruence between class and field, and another school that commented that the plan whereby all of first-year field instruction and approximately 85-90 percent of second-year are under the auspices of full-time faculty has "effected a kind of fusion of class and field that we believe goes beyond what we had formerly discussed as integration."

One school mentioned a community planning seminar as an example of efforts to achieve integration of class and field in the area of community planning. Its purpose was to "provide learning opportunities that will enable students (1) to become more knowledgeable about and familiar with community organization and community planning concepts and issues through direct observation and study; (2) to develop a sense of commitment to the importance of broad social change efforts by the social work profession; and (3) to make meaningful connections between social casework and the wider professional context of social work and social welfare practice in the community-at-large."

Mention was made of the work of the field consultants with field instructors as geared toward integration of class and field. Another way of achieving integration is having school-based faculty do field teaching in the school while the agency field instructor carries administrative responsibility for student assignments.

SUMMARY

In summarizing the changes that have taken place or are contemplated, certain terms can be said to be indicators of change and movement. Without establishing any order of priority, these seem to be social problems, social responsibility, social systems, group, cluster of agencies, cluster of students, (students from several placements clustered together in some sections of casework and human behavior), and community. Possibly the word "group" appears more frequently than any other in the context of modification in learning objectives, conceptualization of field curriculum, learning experiences, and teaching methods. There is group teaching, group learning, and peer learning. Observation, observing, and being observed appear with regularity in descriptions. Apprenticeship is used only in a pejorative sense. Schools universally report a lag in working with agency administrators and regard this as a serious problem. The continuum of modifications extends from new models, such as a 16-month curriculum, teaching centers, or a social-problem focus to questions as to whether there should be any modification or rather a more effective use of existing patterns.

What of the field work of the 1990's into which Gardner propelled us two years ago? Apprenticeship may still be with us but in a far more sophisticated form. It will approximate the description of Kindelsperger, "a major learning pattern that should be carefully controlled."[10] This new pattern, with faculty-advising models, will be developed in teaching centers and "sections" and "community units" as formulated in the truly innovative plans now underway. There will be increasing involvement of students in working out educational programs in the field as, for example, a three-way conference of student, field instructor, and advisor mentioned by a school concerned about present modes of advising. Field instructors will have a less ambiguous role, the outline of which can be seen in the work of at least two schools. A role and status, rank, and promotion comparable to that of full-time class faculty are clearly forecast.

Theoretical formulations for learning and teaching will draw more heavily on social systems and transactional theory than on behavioral theories. An adaptation of the Tyler framework utilizing the principles of continuity, progression, and integration but avoiding the mechanistic detailing of behavioral expectations might be foreseen, as well as use of crisis theory in relation to those points, or peaks and depressions, in learning seen as critical for change in patterns of learning, growth, and development.

Will the persistent questions about the necessity of field practice and the apparent incompatibility of education and service be finally resolved? Will we continue to have proposals for virtual abolishment of field work? It would seem that these questions will linger, but they will not be as troubling to us because of the educational controls set for

---

[10] Walter L. Kindelsperger, "Responsible Entry Into the Profession," *Journal of Education for Social Work*, Vol. 2, No. 1 (Spring, 1966), p. 48.

field learning and teaching, and because we will have settled the meaning of "responsible entry into the profession." Perhaps Ruth Smalley's distinction between the field placement as "locus for the student to apply his knowledge" and "opportunity to develop skill in giving a service"[11] may help us to clarify the essential function of field learning and teaching. We may also learn that field work is not "ungovernable" if we can separate the fundamentals of curriculum from management. Somehow we do arrange courses and we are able to put students and instructors together with a degree of order. The variables in the field are far greater in number than those usually encountered in the class, but we can no longer take refuge in this defense. Some schools with conviction about the necessity of field practice are showing ways to permit the essentials in learning and teaching to assume their priority. It is an ironic note that the ideal of equality has been slow in reaching field work and that our present desire to give all students comparable experiences will give us the key to more fruitful and effective working relationships with agencies. With this principle guiding the "partnership," school and agency may be able to develop together educationally focused field work, aware that, although there are other elements in the interacting system —university, government, community, profession—they, class and field faculty, have primary responsibility for shaping and directing the student and directing the student encounter with client, group, community, social problem, or bureaucracy.

A final impression from this limited survey of modifications in field learning and teaching is that the climate now seems favorable for a systematic study of field work. Interest is high in finding ways to solve the problems presented by expanded enrollments with increased pressures on already strained resources in agencies.

Transcending these practical issues there seems to be an intellectual ferment about field work. It is the right time to take up where the Curriculum Study left field instruction ten years ago, unstudied and unresolved. Field work is in!

---

[11] Ruth Elizabeth Smalley, *Theory for Social Work Practice* (New York: Columbia University Press, 1967), p. 296.

INNOVATIONS IN FIELD LEARNING AND TEACHING

MARK P. HALE

AMONG THE INNOVATIONS introduced in social work education in the past decade, those concerned with field learning or field instruction have assumed increasing significance. Many schools have been involved in trying new approaches to field instruction and relating the field work experience to learning in the classroom. These innovations offer the prospect of enhancing the quality of learning as well as the opportunity for more extensive use of limited resources. Thus, they bear on many of the problems facing social work schools, as they try to respond to such variables as emerging new practice trends, the knowledge and population explosions, the manpower dilemma, and the needs of rapidly expanding social services.

Before these recent innovations in field learning and teaching are analyzed, the context in which they are taking place should be clarified. An innovation is something new. We need, therefore, to know new in relation to what, if we are to understand the change. Likewise, in order to assess the implications of the change, we must look at the forces that have precipitated the innovations or the conditions to which they are addressed. What, then, is being changed in the recent innovations in field learning?

THE TRADITIONAL MODEL

These innovations have all introduced change in the field work model that schools have used for many years. At the risk of oversimplification

MARK P. HALE is director of The Jane Addams Graduate School of Social Work, University of Illinois. This paper was presented at the Council on Social Work Education Fifteenth Annual Program Meeting in Salt Lake City, Utah, January, 1967, and later published in the Social Work Education Reporter, *Vol. 15, No. 3 (September, 1967), pp. 20 ff.*

and overgeneralization, this model—the traditional pattern—might be characterized as follows for purposes of this analysis:[1]

1. The focus is on development of practice skill in some one method of practice.
2. Field learning and class learning proceed concurrently with relatively early introduction of the student to case-carrying, service-giving responsibilities and learning experiences. Some schools intersperse the class and field learning at regular intervals, using a system of "block" placement in agencies.
3. The field learning experiences are based primarily in the agency where the student is placed.
4. The learning experiences are organized and directed by the agency's function and the service needs of the clients included in the student's caseload.
5. The primary teaching-learning method is the tutorial or individual conference based on relationship and role identification with the chief mentor—the field instructor.
6. Work components in the experience are high, inasmuch as the student is expected to perform the work role of an employee in accord with the agency's policies and procedures.

This model has evolved over many years. In general, it has been supported by faculties as an effective learning system. More recently, however, there has been mounting concern about its ready adaptability and viability for the future. As faculties have been engaged in developing long-run plans for expansion and qualitative enhancement of their programs and establishing priorities for these plans, many have become more aware of potential obstacles in the traditional model in relation to these. Innovations and experimentation with some of the conditions and methods of the model have recently suggested ways of overcoming or avoiding possible deficiencies. Before we move to a discussion of such changes, however, a summary of some of the concerns many have with the traditional pattern may be useful. These are not elaborated, since they have been developed in the literature over the past decade or more.[2]

---

[1] For a more extensive description, see Mary Lewis, Dorothy Howerton, and Walter Kindelsperger, *An Experimental Design for First Year Field Instruction* (New Orleans: Tulane University, 1962), pp. 24-28; Margaret S. Schubert, "Curriculum Policy Dilemmas in Field Instruction," *Journal of Education for Social Work*, Vol. 1, No. 2 (Fall, 1965), pp. 35-46; and Mark P. Hale, "The Parameters of Agency-School Social Work Educational Planning," *Journal of Education for Social Work*, Vol. 2, No. 1 (Spring, 1966), pp. 32-40.

[2] See, in addition to references cited above, Katherine A. Kendall, "Selected Issues in Field Instruction in Education for Social Work," *Social Service Review*, Vol. 33, No. 1 (March, 1959), and Mildred Sikkema, "A Proposal For An Innovation in Field Learning and Teaching," *Field Instruction in Graduate Social Work Education: Old Problems and New Proposals* (New York: Council on Social Work Education, 1966).

Again, in the interests of brevity, this précis runs the risk of oversimplification and overgeneralization.

ISSUES AND PROBLEMS

First of these concerns is the question of avoiding a too-narrow focus with the resultant imbalance of learning in the field, or, to put it in the language of standards, how to assure students an opportunity for "diversity and breadth" in field learning as well as "new knowledge and understanding in all content areas of the curriculum."[3] The traditional field work model is not always able to meet such conditions. Highly specialized agencies serving particular kinds of clients may not have a sufficient range of experiences to offer. Such circumstances may be aggravated where the student is only intermittently in the agency and the learning experiences are organized primarily around case-carrying responsibilities. Many agencies, for example, may have very limited opportunities to offer the student in community work, group work, or research. The attachment of the student only to such agencies, therefore, often restricts learning opportunities primarily to one method of practice and the human growth and behavior area of the curriculum. Thus, the field learning experience is denied in some parts of the curriculum, causing an imbalance in learning for the student.

The second problem is one of avoiding the possible bad side effects on student behavior that come from apprenticeship teaching and early case-carrying responsibilities. On one hand, if our concurrent field learning confronts students with responsibility for service to clients before they are ready, the integration of learning can be negatively affected. Yet integration is one of the chief aims we set for field learning. In such circumstances, the student must operate on the field mentor's practice wisdom and knowledge, not his own understanding and knowledge. This can create or overstimulate dependency, with serious consequences on adult learners. The question is how to promote responsible learning and develop student initiative, creativity, and independence.[4]

The third issue is how to minimize or resolve the dichotomy our system generates between the two parts: the field and the class.[5] It involves maintaining the most effective balance and timing possible between the knowledge base and practice or skill components in professional educa-

---

[3] *Manual of Accrediting Standards* (New York: Council on Social Work Education, 1965), Appendix I, p. 59.

[4] Lewis, *et. al., op. cit.,* p. 9.

[5] Schubert, *op. cit.*

23

tion, of helping the student "integrate and balance the intellectual and relationship components of the professional role."[6]

The fourth and final problem is the increasing imbalance between the demand for education and educational resources and the difficulties inherent in expanding and changing our programs to meet increased enrollment and new expectations for learning. Student population and enrollment are increasing faster than faculty, space, and field placements, and will undoubtedly continue to do so. Despite this, schools need to expand enrollments on the order of three or four times in the next decade.[7] Of particular import is the question of integrating the concerns of a service-giving agency with those of an educational institution, taking into consideration the student's learning needs, the role of the agency field instructor, and space. The latter factors—space and supervision —are particularly acute as service demands mount steadily and agencies expand their staffs to meet the service needs of more and more clients. At the same time, schools request more student placements and a wider range of learning experiences and opportunities for students.

THE PATTERNS OF INNOVATION

Within this context of the traditional model and some of the concerns expressed about it, what are the changes the innovations and experiments have introduced? What are their implications for our teaching-learning system in the field?

The following summary is based on innovations that have been followed in more than a dozen schools. It is interesting to note that most of them emerged in these schools at about the same time and with little or no relationship to each other. Thus, they represent the thinking of a good many faculty members about the problems already outlined. The similarity in their response suggests some degree of validity, at least on the grounds of reason, logic, and educational principles. Only recently has there been some degree of formal interchange on an organized basis among some of these faculties. A considerable amount of informal exchange went on among individuals which, although it was not regular or sustained, nevertheless did influence plans and thinking. The School of Social Work at Tulane University has, for the last decade, been con-

---

[6] Walter L. Kindelsperger and Helen Cassidy, *Social Work Training Centers: Tentative Analysis of the Structure and Learning Environment* (New Orleans: Tulane University, 1966), p. 6.

[7] U.S. Department of Health, Education, and Welfare, *Closing the Gap in Social Work Manpower*, Report of the Departmental Task Force on Social Work Education and Manpower (Washington, D. C.: Office of Undersecretary, 1965).

ducting experiments, recording and evaluating results, and using a number of different innovative procedures. Their leadership in trying these changes, while preserving the dual role and balance between field and class learning, has influenced many of the other schools. Their faculty has also paid particular attention to learning theory as it relates to field learning. Some of the innovations in the schools have not been reported in published form, and accounts of them are available only in mimeographed releases based on papers read at meetings.

Since, in this account, these innovations are not reviewed one by one or in detail (an obvious impossibility), the analysis will undoubtedly fail to do justice to the creativity and innovative reach of individuals and schools. As justification, the author pleads lack of time but not lack of recognition of the contributions individuals and schools have made in moving the field forward toward better learning for students and more productive use of limited educational resources.

The innovations that are reviewed seem to reflect five basic revisions of the traditional model. These are:

1. A change in focus.
2. Use of a wider range of learning experiences than usual.
3. Use of more variety in teaching methods in the field.
4. Reliance on a wider range of learning and educational principles and practice theory.
5. Various ways of structuring and organizing the system.

Not all of the innovations reflect all of these changes; some include only one or two.

Change in Focus—Several of the innovations focus on the curriculum and learning needs of the student, not on cases served. In these schools, particular assignments or experiences specifically reflect all curriculum areas and specifically reinforce learning from the classroom through the medium of student interaction with people and clients, and live situations in the field. Experiences in more than one practice method are involved. Several other schools provide for such a focus less explicitly, but not less directly. Another "pilot project" stresses the use of knowledge in the field rather than practice skill, and experiences are designed to accomplish this purpose. A third emphasis is on enhancement of independence or self-directed activity on the part of the student. One school uses the phrase "education for autonomous practice" to describe this focus.[8] Here again, several innovations imply such a goal if not stating it explicitly. Changed teaching methods are viewed as enhancing this focus in several instances. A fourth direction concentrates on the

---

[8] Virginia Franks, "The Autonomous Social Worker," *An Occasional Paper,* No. 1 (Madison, Wisconsin: University of Wisconsin, 1967), a paper presented at the Council on Social Work Education Fourteenth Annual Program Meeting in New York City, January, 1966.

problems of people, the community structure within which these problems are handled, and intervention alternatives for social workers.

These goals do not indicate that all attention to skill is being replaced but rather that such attention is frequently a matter of emphasis or degree and balance. All schools maintain the same general goal that is usually stated—namely, the graduation of students who can begin to assume responsibility for skilled, understanding, and knowledgeable service to people.

WIDER RANGE OF LEARNING EXPERIENCES

The second way these innovations are changing field learning is through the use of a wider range of learning experiences for students. Case-carrying, service-giving learning is not the major learning experience in some semesters or quarters in some of these schools. All do, however, include such experiences for students at some point in their education. Other experiences include observation and study with written analysis and discussions of a wide variety of situations such as interviews, therapy sessions, group life at all ages, decision-making sessions, family interaction, people at play, stress situations, etc. Other experiences include performance of task-oriented or limited service functions, e.g., serving as aide to a group leader in a play school, interviewing an applicant to arrange a camp experience for a child, "friendly visiting" with aged people, taking a medical history, etc. Case reading and analysis is a third general experience. Group reports and discussions of field learning experiences are common. Visits to institutions and services with specific observational, analytical, and assessment assignments are often included. Interviewing professionals about their roles and services and group analysis of student-taped interviews or one-way screen observations are additional experiences used in some innovations. These examples do not exhaust all the experiences. They are only suggestive of what schools may develop as alternatives to sole or major reliance on case-carrying (service-giving) as the chief vehicle for organizing and directing student learning in the field.

Different Teaching Methods—The third change most of the innovations make is in teaching method. Most use group methods more extensively, if not as the major teaching approach. As one school stated, "In the experimental [unit], group instruction was supplemented by individual instruction; in the traditional [units] the reverse was true."[9] In some instances, individual conferences were not regularly scheduled but were held only on an "as needed basis" on the request of the student

---

[9] Lewis, *et. al., op. cit.,* p. 49. See also, Margaret Schubert, *Field Instruction In Social Casework* (Chicago: University of Chicago Press, 1963).

or instructor.[10] Another device used is the "unit caseload" where "all students . . . are responsible for all phases of casework with the client except the actual giving of treatment to the client."[11] This was assigned to one student with the help of the field instructor. Another pedagogical device used is rotation among instructors and services, e.g., in a medical setting. A fourth is joint learning with other professional learners, e.g., with medical students in a medical setting or residents in psychiatry and psychology in a psychiatric setting. A fifth is the teaching of a range of intervention techniques and methods in settings that use more than one method, using consultants or multiple teachers as needed.[12] Use of a coordinator to oversee general aspects of student learning where several different field teachers had responsibility for specific aspects of students' experiences is another procedure followed.[13] Others include demonstrations by experienced professionals of interviewing, treatment, intervention techniques, etc.; use of one-way screens; closed-circuit television to facilitate observation; use of delay of case-carrying and progression in learning to enhance learning and promote independence.

DIFFERENT LEARNING PRINCIPLES AND PRACTICE THEORY

Learning by doing is still used in the innovations, as is learning through relationship and other tested precepts of our usual way of conducting field learning. To these, the innovations add greater reliance on formalizing peer group learning, broader application of role theory, and the structuring of learning experiences on the basis of "levels of social interaction."[14] Greater attention is given to student readiness for, and progression through, the different kinds and levels of learning experiences in order to enhance learning and integration of the total educational experience in both class and field.[15] In order to provide students

---

[10] For one example, see Minna Green Duncan, "An Experiment in Applying New Methods in Field Work," *Social Casework,* Vol. 44 (April, 1963), reprinted in *Trends in Field Work Instruction* (New York City: Family Service Association of America, 1966), p. 36.

[11] Lewis, *et. al., op. cit.,* pp. 45-46.

[12] See, for example, Dorothy Sumner, "An Experiment With Field Work in Generic Social Work," *Social Casework,* Vol. 37 (June, 1956), reprinted *op. cit.,* p. 23. Also Margaret L. Schutz, "Report of the Field Instruction Experimental Project of the George Warren Brown School of Social Work," presented at the Council on Social Work Education Fourteenth Annual Program Meeting, New York City, January, 1966.

[13] Kindelsperger and Cassidy, *op. cit.,* p. 15.

[14] Kindelsperger and Cassidy, *op. cit.,* pp. 15-17.

[15] For example, Schutz, *op. cit.,* pp. 12-19.

with a better cognitive learning base before they assumed service-giving responsibilities, the assignment of cases for continuing service was often delayed for a term or semester. Some of the innovations also introduce students to a wider range of practice theory that encompasses not only the psychoanalytic and ego psychology frames of reference, but also group theory, role theory, transactional and environment theories, and other behavioral and social science concepts useful in a variety of intervention situations and patterns.[16]

Organizational Changes—The final change the innovations make is in the organization of field learning. Traditionally this has been done by basing the student in an agency where he begins to assume the practitioner function of that agency and service. Many of the innovations cut loose from this pattern. They base units in a community and use all agencies in that community for learning experiences. They organize experiences around a set of problems and services for them, e.g., child welfare or the aged. They base students in a neighborhood or medical complex. They use an institutional-wide complex for mental health. Out of such organizational patterns has come the use of the teaching center combining numerous student units and instructors and thus greatly facilitating the broader teaching focus, diversity in learning experiences, and other teaching methods noted earlier. Tulane's account of two such centers should be required reading for all faculties of schools interested in field innovation.[17]

Another aspect of organization is experimentation with the size of the teaching unit in the field. Some innovations use ten instead of the more typical seven or eight students per unit. There is some evidence that 12 may be a more productive learning group, and even larger units for certain experiences may be possible. Unit size is, of course, a factor in determining teaching methods and kinds of learning experiences.

IMPLICATIONS OF THE INNOVATIONS

With this overgeneralized description of the patterns of innovation, we can now examine their import. What implications do they have for the future of our programs in field learning? Do they offer better ways of field learning? Do they bear significantly on the problems noted earlier? Before we look at these questions, it should be noted that, in those instances where formal testing of outcomes was done, the level of achievement of the experimental students was as high or higher than

---

[16] *Ibid.*, pp. 9-11. Also see William E. Gordon, "Toward a Social Work Frame of Reference," *Journal of Social Work Education*, Vol. 1, No. 2 (Fall, 1965), pp. 19-26.

[17] Lewis, *et. al.* See also Sikkema, *op. cit.*

the control group. Where clinical observations of experienced field instructors were the only evaluation used, similar outcomes were noted. In other words, changes in the structure and nature of field learning do not appear to affect negatively student performance. In fact, the evidence is to the contrary.

In this writer's view, these innovations offer social work education an opportunity not only to enhance the quality of learning, but also to use limited educational resources to accommodate more learners. They demonstrate that field learning can be standardized and broadened for all students to a greater extent than in the traditional system. All students can achieve a common base of knowledge and skill in more areas of the curriculum by use of field learning for the total curriculum. Thus, learning can be better balanced between the several methods and the other curriculum areas.

These innovations demonstrate that the full range of experiences offered by a community can be made available to students. Services not heretofore used because of absence of supervisory talent, space limitations, etc., may now be incorporated into a community or problem-based learning center or used in ways other than for primary student placements.

The innovations also focus attention more on the learner's situation and needs in developing learning experiences. Thus, they can adapt the pace and experiences to the student's ability to learn rather than to the imperatives of agency or client, and avoid much of the behavioral bad side effects with which field teachers constantly deal in the traditional system. Accordingly, they hold the prospect of producing a more independent, self-directed, knowledgeable practitioner for the future. They are less bound to agency practice at a given time, and may be more adaptable to orientation to future practice.

The innovations also offer more productive use of valuable, limited teaching personnel. By cutting loose from sole dependence on a single agency base for all field learning, they suggest solutions to the space problems many schools now face in field learning.

Finally, the innovations seem to offer an opportunity to strengthen educational theory and principles for broader and more effective learning. There is the prospect of enhanced integration of the knowledge base and practice components in the curricula. They also introduce greater unity and coherence into the total curriculum.

Earl McGrath's analysis of the relation of general education to professional education notes a number of stages of growth through which professional educational programs tend to progress. The final and most effective of these is that of full integration of liberal education with specialization in the science of the profession. This stage is characterized by a shift in "emphasis from a narrow preoccupation with technical details and how-to-do-it skills to broad subject matter"; stress on "the analytical intellectual processes required to prepare the student

29

adequately for his professional activities"; and, "core courses in the professional field stressing principles rather than details of fact and technique."[18]

The innovations reviewed here seem to be consistent with such a stage of development for social work education—a stage in which knowledge and its practical application are combined to achieve the highest degree of development of independent professional practice skill; a stage that can keep pace with new developments and new knowledge as they emerge in the profession.

---

[18] Earl J. McGrath, *Liberal Education in the Professions* (New York: Institute of Higher Education, Columbia University Teachers College, 1959), pp. 28-34.

PART II
SETTINGS AND PRACTICE
METHODS

INTEGRATING PRACTICE DEMANDS IN SOCIAL WORK EDUCATION

CAROL H. MEYER

NOT LONG ago social work education conferences were concerned with such topics as coordinating agency and school practice modes and fitting the graduate into agency molds. The tie to apprenticeship training was discernible in the choice of topic. Perhaps, then, today's interest in finding ways to incorporate the demands of practice into the educational structure is an indication of social work's growth as a profession.

The current structure of social work education rests on an assumption that may require scrutiny, however, if progress is to be made in solving the venerable problem of town and gown. The assumption is that the schools, in their educational programs, and the agencies, in their practice programs, exhibit similar, if not identical, commitments to the service role of social work in the community. It is assumed that the school and the agency are concerned with the same ultimate goals and that social work education and practice are more or less integrated.

EXAMINATION OF ASSUMPTIONS

Although these assumptions may have been valid in the past, they appear less so at the present time for several reasons: (1) Social workers in schools and agencies do not always agree on what the concerns of the social work profession should be. (2) The community has begun to encroach upon the professional stance in regard to practice. The

CAROL H. MEYER is a professor at the Columbia University School of Social Work. Her article is based on a paper presented at the Sixteenth Annual Program Meeting of the Council on Social Work Education held in Minneapolis, Minnesota, January, 1968. This article was originally published in Social Casework, Vol. 49, No. 8 (October, 1968), pp. 481-486. Reprinted with permission.

actual or intended recipients of service are indicating in many ways that social workers may be doing something wrong, and that the faculty of schools, the administrators of agencies, and the individual workers hear the criticisms differently and respond to them idiosyncratically. (3) Social work knowledge evolves unevenly—sometimes through research, sometimes through theory development, and sometimes through practice experience in various stages of articulation. Thus, while agency staffs may be experimenting with advanced forms of family treatment, faculty members may be finding it difficult to identify the significant concepts of family treatment that can be taught in the classroom. On the other hand, the developmental level of some theories, such as social systems theory, may still be too abstract for immediate transfer from the classroom to practice. (4) Agencies are accountable for performing an immediate function, whereas schools are obligated to educate for future practice. (5) Despite the schools' and agencies' total commitment to generic social work education, the specifics of agency practice are so varied that it is impossible to prepare students thoroughly for the variables of all fields of practice. Because of variations in organizational, cultural, and geographical factors affecting agency practice, as well as differences in emphasis for several kinds of client groupings, it can be said that it is an accident today when a graduate of a school of social work is prepared to practice in accordance with the demands of a particular agency.

The above issues seem to undermine any assurance that schools and agencies have identical missions in social work, or even that they have identical perceptions of their roles. Despite such obstacles to mutuality, however, the social work system is still sufficiently flexible to allow different emphases to exist. Schools and agencies do agree, however, that the social work profession must somehow more effectively carry out the public's mandate and that students must be prepared to advance practice. The student as a potential professional practitioner, therefore, may be a more appropriate focus for the purpose of this discussion. Moreover, if educators and practitioners can agree to join efforts to educate the social work student for the future, the temptation to train the student in their own images may be avoided.

THE FUTURE OF PRACTICE

Social workers cannot discuss proposals for the improvement of social work education without being concerned with the content of future practice. For, just as efficient recording flows from effective practice and skilled interviewing results from sound understanding of the client, so educational processes are only as relevant as is the conception of practice. All social workers do not view the future in the same way, however. Some workers perceive the future as existing in the present and, therefore, regard as irrelevant all questions about the efficacy of current practice. Obviously, the realities of practice are directly encountered in the field agencies, while reality is seen in the schools through the screen of many agencies, all of which have different views. Jurisdictional disputes resulting from the different standpoints can be minimized, however, if the parameters of practice and the resultant education for practice are defined. This task can be accomplished by using available data on recent population trends, both statistical and ecological; on the nature and intensity of modern social problems; on the availability of current staff to carry out practices; and on the effectiveness of a traditional methodology.

Several formulations concerning the future of social work practice may be derived from the evidence at hand. The socio-economic data indicate that ours is an urban society of increasing population density. The members of such a society will have to rely more heavily on social institutions and money income than on extended family supports and earning a living from the land. The social services that are rapidly becoming the source of such suprafamily help and the bridge between families and all other social institutions will have to depend on diversely trained personnel if the community's mandate is to be carried out. Furthermore, social work methodology will have to be made functional for its time through new modes of case finding and coverage and of supplying rapid help. When the social scene is viewed in this manner, certain implications for social work education logically follow.

THE TEACHING CENTER

Some faculty members of the Columbia University School of Social Work, convinced of the soundness of such a view of the social scene, had begun to question the functional value of assigning to casework students, for their learning in field work, only six or eight carefully selected cases during the academic year. They questioned the readiness of students to break out of rigid, compartmentalized practice modes when they had not been exposed to group work and to community organization practices. They supported the idea that students need to learn the differential use of nonprofessional staff. Also, because they knew that many graduates are quickly made responsible for program planning, as well as for direct service, they doubted the advisability of teaching methodological skills in a social policy and administrative vacuum. The timing of the questions and the doubts was fortunate because the school had recently agreed to administer, as a teaching center, the social service department of a large, unstructured city hospital situated in a ghetto area of New York.

The hospital provided an advantageous educational experience because the existing social work services were far from adequate and any service provided by the students, whether innovative or traditional, was

35

greatly needed. In addition, there was no existing structure rigid enough to confine the students' activities or the administration of the student program. The hospital was a small "community" in its own right. It served as a medical and psychiatric center for the entire area and, except for the public welfare department, provided the only professional social service program for the residents. Consequently, people in the neighborhood needed social work help, and innovative programs were welcomed. Fortunately, a courageous, competent caseworker, who had experience in community organization, was the field instructor. The opportunity that was presented seemed to be a field work dream come true; one could begin from the beginning and devise an innovative educational-service program under any conceptual scheme deemed relevant.

At the present time, several schools of social work are experimenting by organizing field work as an extension of classwork. The students involved in such programs are not assigned to a particular agency, but rather to a teaching center from which they may go to any one of many agencies. The assignments are not based on the needs of the service settings; they are determined by a sequence of experiences geared to an academic sequence of principles. In this way, the problem of integrating classroom learning and field practice learning is "solved" by making the latter an extension of the former, rather than an entity with demands and dynamics of its own. In the hospital, however, the program and the experiences for learning developed from an appraisal of the needs of the setting as well as the needs and wishes of the clients. The program was designed to be setting-centered, but the view of the needed services transversed pre-existing methodological boundaries, staffing patterns, and field teaching. The program for the student unit was shaped by a willingness to look afresh at the needs of people in relation to their neighborhoods and the hospital; by the educational needs of students; and by the creativity of the school, the field instructor, and the students in making a service and training program come alive in operation.

THE RATIONALE FOR THE UNIT

The unit was called the Family and Child Welfare Unit, and the rationale for its functioning was based on the following assumptions:

1. In view of the increasing demand for social work graduates, the scarcity of professional practitioners will continue. Practitioners, therefore, need to know how to use and work with variously trained nonprofessional staff members.

2. The community expects professional practitioners to be independent, responsible, and able to handle the complicated organizational problems that are of a larger dimension than the individual case. Therefore, the professional practitioner needs to know how to

differentiate among multiple pressures—to sort out priorities and determine which clients need direct, intensive help and which clients need concrete services or referrals elsewhere. He must also have skills in management of a caseload, as well as treatment skills.

3. The fusion of methods, or at least techniques, seems inevitable. Therefore, students need opportunities to learn other method skills, as well as casework skills; they need to know when one or another or a combination of all methods is indicated.

4. New modes are being developed for early intervention, case finding, and attention to crisis or stress periods. Students can learn such practice modes within the limited "community" of the hospital structure and be prepared in knowledge and skills.

The student who completes an educational experience based on such assumptions should be prepared for the real world of casework practice in public welfare agencies, neighborhood service centers, schools, hospitals, family courts, or any community-based child welfare or family agency or psychiatric clinic.

EVALUATION OF THE EXPERIENCE

In the first year, four of the five students were second-year students who, therefore, brought to the placement some basic casework experience. The students had average or above-average grades, and the principal determinant for their selection was *their* interest in the project and their faculty advisor's imagination and consent. All the students had performed well in their first-year classes and field practice. It may be said that the dice were loaded inasmuch as all were bright students and had excellent supervision. Conceivably, the aphorism also applies to the conception of the unit, for if the social scene and the related function of social work services were perceived correctly, how could the program fail?

The students found their own cases through the clinics and the wards and, in a few instances, on the street outside the hospital. They carried almost 40 cases on all levels of casework treatment. They worked at developing group services for fathers in their combined caseloads and for children confined to wards. The group services program did not work out well in the first year, and a different and more aggressive approach was tried in the second year. The students conducted a community action and research project related to the high incidence of asthma in their caseloads. They involved the schools and the public health stations in a study of the prevalence of the illness. They recommended specific action programs for the treatment of the acute stage of asthma in children. Each of the second-year students supervised a nonprofessional worker who was being trained by the Women's Talent Corps, an organization engaged in the training of aides in the fields of social service, education, and health. In the hospital program, the women worked under the direction of the students, performing selected tasks for the students' clients and serving as recreational assistants in the children's wards. An evaluation process conducted by the students with the women became a major learning experience in itself.

Much had been learned in the first year about the untapped possibilities for student training in a teaching center, and in the second year the program was expanded. The students carried the total social service program in the pediatric, allergy, neurology, and obesity clinics and, for a short time, in an emergency clinic. They kept track of the patients, attempting to see everyone in order to make differential diagnoses and emergency treatment plans. In addition, each student supervised one or two nonprofessional Women's Talent Corps workers. The community action program in the second year was focused on preparing two child health stations for more extensive co-operative work with the medical services of the hospital and the social work services of the neighborhood; for this program, the students conducted, among their other tasks, more than 380 interviews with mothers in the community.

The group work service projects consisted of educational and activity groups of obese children and a ward of hospitalized children. In addition, each student carried an ongoing caseload of seven, eight, or nine cases and was responsible for formulating complete psychosocial diagnoses and treatment plans. Throughout the academic year, the students worked with the medical staff of the pediatrics division and participated in the psychiatric seminars for students.

It may be impossible to detect all the serendipitous results of the student program. Who can evaluate its significance to the patients served, for example, or to the doctors who learned that it was unwise to discharge a patient before obtaining the social worker's knowledge of the family's readiness to receive him? Insofar as the students are concerned, a questionnaire was sent to the students involved in the first year of the experiment in order to determine the effect of the unit experience on their current practice. Three of the graduates were working in public welfare agencies. They found great similarities between the client groups served in their agencies and in the hospital, and they were convinced of the necessity of providing a flexible range of social work services and of carrying a highly responsible professional role in service delivery. It had not surprised them to find that the agencies, although interested, were not prepared to break down methodological barriers, to use nonprofessional personnel differentially, or to provide opportunities for imaginative and innovative practices, and they did feel somewhat frustrated. The fourth graduate was employed by the hospital. In a sense, his work was a continuation of the demonstration student unit program, and yet it was decidedly different. His role as a professional was more structured and traditional than it had been as a student. The former first-year student was doing his second-year field work in a private, suburban family agency and was relieved to be in a more protected setting. He recommended assigning only second-year students who have mastered basic casework skills to experimental student units.

AREAS OF CONTROVERSY

The last recommendation is related to the questions that may be asked concerning the limitations of such experimental units as the Family and Child Welfare Unit. One probable question is how can students assigned to the hospital unit be as well-prepared as others in the clinical component of casework treatment when the spread of their educational experience has been so wide as to include group services and community services, program planning, caseload management, research, and supervision of nonprofessional personnel? Part of the answer to this question lies in the evaluation of the effectiveness of clinical expertise in casework. It is possible that some of the notable failures that have been described in recent social work studies are not related to expertise but to the quality of the research itself. Perhaps the proper research tools for evaluating treatment effectiveness have not yet been devised. On the other hand, there is question whether clinical expertise alone is sufficient for social casework practice.

A review of what is currently known about need may help to clarify the issue. Our urban society is one in which socio-economic problems seem to infiltrate the lives not only of poor persons in the ghettos but also of all other persons who must cope with the tensions, the confusions, and the sense of isolation that pervade urban life. Furthermore, for a host of reasons, personality manifestations are very different today from what they were 20 years ago. Formerly, persons with neurotic conflicts applied for clinical services. At present, the prevailing clinical syndrome is called the acting-out character disorder. Social workers know that this term is imprecise and that additional psychological, sociological, and economic knowledge is required to describe clients more accurately. As social work's diagnostic parameters enlarge, so must its treatment modalities. Whereas, one-to-one interviews were once considered the ultimate in effectiveness, we know now that joint interviews and family interviews may be more useful, and current treatment plans often include the use of welfare client organizations, group methods, and community action by the client in his own behalf. Moreover, since treatment is more frequently carried out by nonprofessionals than by professionals, ways of allotting tasks appropriately need to be devised. The clinical expertise some social workers may still be seeking has, in itself, changed; the clinic has moved outdoors, and its shape is being redrawn.

Another part of the answer to the question of whether students must first master a primary method, such as casework, before expanding their practice education, lies in one's view of the learning process itself. Students learn from repetition and reinforcement, from generalization, and from conceptualization. Consequently, students should have more, not less, cases from which to learn in order to repeat their skills. They should have variety in their experiences in order to observe similarities that will reinforce each other. They should gain awareness of the broad scheme in which their own practice fits in order to generalize. They should also be able to communicate to others, such as nonprofessional staff, the meanings of what they are learning as an aid to conceptualization. In other words, there are primary educational values for students in learning about the total social work scheme.

The graduate who has had the kind of educational experience described in this article may encounter resistance when he enters practice. Apparently, many social workers consider it a mixed blessing to have independent, innovative, highly qualified social workers employed by agencies. Traditionally, social work has required probably the longest period of induction known to any profession. In the science of physics, for example, a 25-year-old graduate knows more than his superiors, and a 30-year-old physicist is considered a "has-been." This phenomenon is, of course, the result of the rapid expansion of knowledge in the physical sciences. Although the knowledge explosion in social work is not up to the level of that in the physical sciences, renovations in knowledge are taking place, and the view of society and the definitions of social work practice are changing radically. Creative, young social workers may not choose to adapt to traditional practices unless the practices are relevant to today's society. It is, however, the primary function of the university to open minds and to provide the analytic tools with which students will probe in their practice. It is not the function of the university to train students to adapt to practice as it is. Graduates whose minds are open may indeed challenge the established modes of practice, but if educators and practitioners achieve a tolerant and welcoming attitude, the profession will benefit in the long run.

DISCUSSION

Dr. MEYER's excellent paper is a boon to a discussant because of the clarity with which she outlines her assumptions and describes the competence that the students achieved through a particular and desirable learning experience in field instruction. In responding from an agency perspective, it is not possible to speak for all agencies, or even for practice as opposed to education, since each is involved in the other. Nevertheless, agency administrators and supervisors often express reservations concerning the competence of newly graduated workers, and their reservations are sometimes different from those expressed by other practitioners.

Young people, naturally, are impatient with the expectation that a broad range of knowledge and judgment should guide professional intervention. They feel they are ready for action based upon whatever they already know. This attitude presents a real challenge to the schools: to hold to an insistence upon what a professional person needs to *know* in order to *do*, and to present a knowledge base of such relevance and immediacy that its applicability to professional action will be unquestioned.

Field instruction is the arena in which the applicability of knowledge to the development of professional skills comes most prominently to the fore. Here the schools, the agencies, and the students are all engaged in the process of putting together the elements of tomorrow's practice.

Dr. Meyer presents for scrutiny the assumption that schools and agencies have similar, if not identical, commitments to the service role of social work, and she questions whether the assumption is valid at the present time. She outlines issues that seem to her to cast doubt and proposes a different base for the joint activities of schools and agencies, selecting, for her purpose, a focus on the future professional practitioner. It seems to me that the issues and the assumptions constitute the most fruitful area for discussion.

Few agency administrators would quarrel with the learning goals that were set for the students in the field unit Dr. Meyer describes, or with the extended kinds of practice assigned to them. Many would agree that there is a necessity, in all field instruction, to seek such a range of learning experiences. What strikes me forcibly is that Dr. Meyer

MARY R. BAKER is director of Personnel Service, Family Service Association of America. This paper was originally published in Social Casework, *Vol. 49, No. 8 (October, 1968), pp. 486-488. Reprinted with permission.*

views the opportunity to create this training center as a "field work dream come true" because it offers a chance to devise an educational-service program without reference to any existing agency structure or purpose. If the schools' mission becomes one not only of preparing the professional practitioner but also of devising the forms of service for which he is prepared, it seems likely that the areas of difference between schools and agencies will increase rather than diminish. Is there an implication that agencies are so static and so rigid that they can no longer render appropriate service? Are the schools unable to locate and utilize the agencies in which the changes in practice are going on? Will the schools increasingly supply their own settings for delivering services through the supervision and administration of student activities? If these activities increasingly differ from the activities of practitioners in the usual service settings, the students face a difficult adjustment in agency employment. If the field instruction objectives Dr. Meyer recommends cannot be attained in agencies, it seems reasonable to question whether the students *are* being socialized into the profession as it exists. Many agencies share the school's concerns and are willing and able to involve themselves in providing field instruction along the lines of extended service. Few agencies, however, receive the kind of investment of a school's imagination, time, and money in devising a field instruction unit within the agency that was given for the hospital unit.

Agency practitioners will find reassurance in Dr. Meyer's discussion of the level of clinical competence with which the students emerged, although they may also have questions. We can readily agree that clinical expertise is not, in itself, the only component of social casework practice, but it is a component without which we cannot do. We will fervently agree that we lack the means to measure the effectiveness of treatment and that we greatly need them, both for agency programs and for the development of knowledge. We accept the description of society and its needs and agree that there is need for enlargement of diagnostic parameters and for a range of treatment modalities. Some of us are convinced that many of the direct service practitioners of the future will not be products of professional social work education; we are less convinced that we know how to divide the treatment process into tasks suitable for professional and agency-trained workers. We want new workers with the ability these students have to understand the total social work scheme, to fit their own practice into it, and to be able to conceptualize their work.

Agency executives and supervisors yearn for clinical practitioners who are competent and prepared for immediate practice, and they will always be less than satisfied. This statement does not imply, however, that they dislike the more broadly prepared graduate who has a firmer base of knowledge and a greater ability to use himself creatively in a variety of situations. I would urge educators to maintain their image of the ideal professional practitioner, but at the same time to remember that a profession cannot be practiced without the methodological skills that are built on a theoretical base and the ability to use a wide range of professional knowledge and judgment. Both in the agency and in the school, we face the problem of giving students confidence in the applicability of what we now know and can do, while freely acknowledging how much we do not know and pointing out the areas in which new knowledge and new skill are most urgently needed.

If educational programs and practice programs are not rooted in a commitment to the service role of social work, I can find no justification for them at all. The adoption of a different assumption does not prevent the polarization of issues that Dr. Meyer wishes to avoid. Pushed to its furthest point, her paper seems to imply that agency practice does not now represent the practice demand in social work and will do so only when it has changed in the directions indicated. I submit that the delivery of social work service is and will continue to be to a large extent through agency programs, that agencies are the places in which most graduates will be employed, and that schools fail in their purpose if they do not produce social workers who meet the demands of such employment. That is not to say that agency services remain fixed and immutable, but rather that graduates need to meet the demands of current programs and that the programs themselves need the knowledge and skill of both old and new workers to change and develop in many new directions.

I should like to comment on each of the issues Dr. Meyer presents as reasons why it is no longer valid to assume a common commitment to the service role. She states them with little or no elaboration, and yet this section of the paper is so thought-provoking that I believe it well may be a definition of the areas in which agencies and schools need to work together to integrate educational experience with practice demands.

1. Uncertainty and disagreement within the whole profession about the nature of social work and the best means for delivery of social work services are of long standing. Are the planners of educational programs now adopting points of view about this that differ from those in the agency? Have our questions and uncertainties ceased to be based on common grounds?

2. Is it true that criticisms voiced by the consumers of the product are more clearly heard in the schools than in the agencies? I believe our clients want our service product and react to the lack of service or the lack of enough kinds of help rather than to the quality of service. Criticism more often comes from persons who want more for the consumers of our service and who blame the profession for failure to mobilize the whole society to supply fundamental needs. Agency staffs believe they are reacting responsibly to the redefinition of needs by various groups in the community, within the inevitable limits of funding

and the impossibility of abandoning all current programs in order to provide new ones. New forms of service, such as the Family and Child Welfare Unit Dr. Meyer describes, may exemplify a desirable restructuring of service programs, but many steps are necessary before agency programs can be reorganized, even if it were conceded that all of them should be. Students who may like such a new organization of service need also to know how and why current service programs developed and what it takes in thought, time, and effort to shift them.

3. Dr. Meyer makes a most important statement about the uneven evolution of knowledge—out of research, out of theory development, and out of practice. By its very nature, this characteristically uneven development seems to me to require more closely identical commitment of schools and agencies to the service role of social work. The evolution of professional knowledge has meaning only in its usefulness for service, if I understand correctly the nature of a profession. Schools and agencies must remain together in pooling the contributions of each to the knowledge base on which both of them rely.

4. The accountability of the agencies for rendering services in the present does not preclude looking ahead to the services of the future. Similarly, the schools' obligation to prepare practitioners who will be adequate for the unknowns of practice 30 years, or even ten years, from now does not relieve them of the obligation to prepare them also for the practice of today. The future will come out of both the education of today's students and their practice in today's and tomorrow's agencies. What we surely must give them is adaptability, an open mind for new knowledge and new problems, and the ability to change and develop.

5. The final issue is the wide variation in practice in the many different kinds of social work agencies, social work functions, and client groupings. Agencies of all kinds, I believe, have accepted the fact that it is impossible to design a curriculum that can educate a worker for such a range of specifics. Further, agencies have accepted the desirability of giving all social workers a common base in fundamental knowledge and understanding of the range of practice. A constant process of testing the graduate in practice, of identifying both the value of things he brings to the agency and the need for things he lacks, must be a basic, shared process between schools and agencies if both are to perform well in their respective spheres. Supervisors and executives may well object to the agency's being the school's locus for teaching a kind of practice that, in fact, does not go on in the agency. And, in the schools, a service setting may have to be developed that exemplifies a form of practice that cannot be found in the field. A profession, however, requires not only the common concern of schools and agencies with its service role but also a willingness to see the preparation of its practitioners validated by their performance in commonly defined professional tasks.

44

NEW SETTINGS FOR GROUP WORK: ON A CLEAR DAY

PAUL ABELS

THE MOTIVE which prompts one to ask "What are the new settings for group work?" is not a desire for idle conversation or satisfaction in seeing group work expand its boundaries of service into additional uncharted waters. The question is asked for more significant reasons, the most vital being: What should we be teaching our students? Are we preparing them for practice that will be relevant to today's problems and needs? Can we predict where group work will be utilized; and, if so, what are the implications for social work education? How can we prepare our students for what we believe will be relevant practice and still equip them to bring about their own changes in the field?

In essence, the question is only significant if it represents a quest for an understanding of client need and the professional assignment so that we can assess how to invest our capital—the prospective social workers. With the limited resources available, we must also determine in which areas the professional is most likely to make his unique contribution. This paper will explore some of the areas in which our investments seem to be heading.

One of the most exciting and potentially fruitful developments is the establishment of "training centers." The Garden Valley Training Center in Cleveland was an attempt to see what might evolve in a learning situation where all three methods could be mobilized to work together on behalf of the client, and where the staff, for the most part, would consist of the students placed in the agency. Under a grant provided by the Children's Bureau, Case Western Reserve University entered into an agreement to use the Garden Valley Neighborhood Center as a resource to help develop new patterns of training and new patterns of service. Garden Valley, although originally a group service agency, over the years had added both casework and community organization programs. The initiation for joint programming between the school and the agency came from Garden Valley, and, under the conditions of the joint effort, both the Welfare Federation and the Presbytery agreed to continue to support the agency financially.

PAUL ABELS is a professor at the School of Applied Social Sciences, Case Western Reserve University. This paper was originally presented at the Council on Social Work Education Sixteenth Annual Program Meeting in Minneapolis, Minnesota, January, 1968.

Garden Valley with its 22 students—seven in casework, 11 in community organization, and four in group work—may offer us not only new experiences and techniques in teaching students in the field, but also expose the students to new approaches to service delivery heretofore merely talked about in teaching situations. They can be exposed to all aspects of service by all the methods involved at the Center, and, perhaps more significantly, can understand the benefits of all the methods working together. The students become partners in the system in which the *providers, consumers, arrangers,* and *payers* of service in a particular undertaking work together toward the solution of the problem. Hopefully in this situation, the student's education will include not only direct delivery of services but also experience in helping others deliver service.

Although it is still in its formative stages, the training center is searching for ways to expose students to the contributions each method has made to the total goals of education and service. Experiments with common training agendas, in which the total student group looks at client problems together, as well as the use of the "social problem approach" to training, which cuts across method lines, illustrate current explorations. Students working with the Maternal-Infant Health Program not only work with mothers' groups, but examine the range of health services available in the community with the goal of changing the patterns of use and availability of services. Students have been free to consult with supervisors from other methods about certain problems and, in fact, have used each other as consultants quite extensively. Immediate plans include assignments in a second method on a formal basis for all the students at the Center.

There is little doubt that in time the students' and the supervisors' mutual exposure to several methods will lead to new ways to help. With this approach to contemplating service for a family concerned about the lack of garbage collection, services from public welfare, poor shopping facilities, or police protection, and their children's behavior, it is hard to believe that we would emerge with the same patterned ways of helping as in the past. The students' excitement and eagerness to be placed in such a setting, when linked to the benefits of this kind of placement, might very well suggest that this may be a highly sought-after experience for many students in the future.

The impact of some 20 students on each other is yet to be determined. The impact on the community and the school has already been felt. The school has had to become directly involved in the problems of the community. Community concerns with the agency have been carried over to concerns with the image and role of the university. The potential for mutual learning and help seems endless.

The desire to expose the group work student to other methods is reflected in other experiments on a lesser scale. Although our primary investment is in professionals who are skilled in the use of groups, there is an attempt to broaden the range of skills and experiences for group work students. One such experience in one of our "new" settings, a half-way house for discharged mental hospital patients, provides the student an opportunity to work with groups, carry an individual client and family, and undertake research on the use of groups. Other broadening experiences include an experiment in which all students in all methods who work with the aged meet monthly as a group to discuss some of their concerns, acquire new knowledge, and test out ideas. Field instructors and faculty advisers join in these meetings, which also include students and faculty from another school of social work. Increasingly there is indication that we are concentrating our services on high-risk groups. These groups need the services of highly skilled and knowledgeable practitioners. If we were to look back just a few years in history to the three classifications of service that Vinter reported in the Detroit study (1) socialization, 2) rehabilitation, and 3) facilities provision),[1] we could state that there is an increase in the placement of students and the use of professionals in the area of rehabilitation (ameliorating social problems and modifying deviance) in its broadest sense.

The turn from a narrow view of socialization as the major area of action for the professional has brought about the task definition and simplification necessary to permit the use of agency-trained workers. This may have resulted in a drop in the skills level thought necessary for work with socialization groups. The social work practitioner needs to concentrate his expertise in those "new" areas involving clients who cannot be helped by agency-trained workers. In time, as our understanding of serving "hard to help" groups becomes institutionalized, the training for helping here, too, may be simplified, and agency-trained workers may assume that helping role as well. Many settings require not only skill in work with groups, but ability to work with and often supervise the agency-trained or indigenous worker. Although some second-year assignments carry supervisory responsibilities, this needs to become institutionalized. The insistent graduate can find an assignment in which he leads a group; but more often than not he will soon be in a supervisory or managerial position. This seems increasingly true for all areas of social work.

For example, one group worker in a child welfare agency was originally hired to set up groups, but she soon found herself more involved in staff training functions than in group work. The needs of the public agencies seem so great that professionals soon find themselves functioning as teachers rather than practitioners—in essence, enabling others to work with groups. Another recent group work graduate starting in child welfare is now doing intake for group homes, working with

---

[1] Robert D. Vinter, "New Evidence for Restructuring Group Service," *New Perspectives on Service to Groups, 1961* (New York: NASW, 1961).

group "home groups," supporting the house parents, and teaching the other staff how to work in similar situations. We recognize that our students are becoming supervisors and managers. Increasingly, our placements are including the opportunity to learn some of the necessary supervisory and management skills which appear to be demanded by most group work practitioners shortly after graduation.

Practice-trends seem to be toward working with those "hard to help" groups having specific problem-solving or goal-directed concerns. These are not the social clubs or the youth groups. They are the welfare mothers' groups and the angry youth groups. They are the tenant union groups, where the groups are not hard to reach, but the goal is.

Some students working with school-referred groups have organized community-wide tutoring programs, working with the tutors and negotiating with teachers, principals, and community groups—in essence, utilizing group leadership, organization, and administrative skills.

Allegations of our over-investment of social work services with the middle class to the detriment of service to the poor are well known; it may suffice to say that there is an obvious increase in emphasizing assignments with the poor. These groups include Head Start mothers, A.D.C., and welfare mothers' groups within Public Welfare, in settlements, and in other settings where similar groups exist or can be formed. A number of students have been assigned to work with school-referred children—potential trouble-makers, potential drop-outs, and potential kick-outs. The settings for these groups have varied from schoolroom to settlement to church, which might indicate that it is not the setting that is important as much as the purpose for the group's existence, and the worker's skills.

Often in these cases the hardest part of the task is to find a setting for which we have a group; to convince an agency that this group can benefit by service, and is, in fact, entitled to service under the agency mandate. Many of these groups may, in a short period of time, become decided risks for the agency as they challenge traditional ways of service and traditional power allocations. This suggests an additional area of change which may take place in group work settings—use of the "risk" agency or "non-agency." It is no secret that agencies with "secure" financing are generally able to find some trained professional staff. It is also no secret that many agencies in which we would like to place students (inner-city agencies, non-agency-sponsored groups such as tenant unions, block clubs, and welfare mothers) are not able to or concerned about recruiting professional staff.

One solution might be to assign the student to a "secure" agency and a "risk" agency or a non-agency, utilizing the skills of the agency with the professionally educated field instructor, and offering a new placement opportunity at the same time the old placement is being used. The student would benefit, the slum group would benefit, and the traditional placement would not only make a contribution of the educational process and to the inner city, but also to its own growth and understanding as well. In the long run, the concept of a unified profession with certain responsibilities to its professional contract may result. The use of limited professional resources necessitates cooperative endeavors if the total society is to be served, and social work is to remain relevant to current social needs.

No longer new, but worth mentioning, are some areas previously neglected by social group workers, public welfare for example. When an area such as this has opened up and those who were willing to risk have shown what can be done, we have subsequently proceeded to offer service. The growth of group work in public welfare has prompted one author to note ". . . the use of social group work in the public assistance programs assumes band wagon proportions. . . ."[2] We should note also the rapid movement by many agencies to use of groups and their "discovery" that the group has certain advantages in some settings, for some people, and for some goals, as an agent of help. Increasingly, in many settings, the group worker will operate as the teacher as well as the direct practitioner, helping others see the value of the group in the change process. More often, he will also be a member of a team with other practitioners in the health fields and also with teachers, city planners, politicians, and lawyers. In these situations he will not only continue to demonstrate his understanding and skills in the use of groups, but will utilize his other skills as well, demanding the involvement of people in decisions that affect their lives, and stressing the need for a therapeutic stance in all efforts in which he is engaged.

Like other professions, we have had to re-evaluate our professional contract. Lawyers have always worked with the poor, and yet it is only in the last few years that they have started to be concerned with the "legal problems of the poor." (At the Western Reserve Law School, for example, such a course was offered this year for the first time.) The poor have always been social work's business, but only recently have we again been able to proclaim, "that is what social work is all about."

I am certain that some of the trends discussed in this paper are occurring in urban areas other than Cleveland. Partly, the changes reflect the nature of the times in which we live, but partly they are the results of the push and pull of the "two cultures of social work." One culture sees the individual as a sick person and generally follows a medical model. The second culture suggests that the problem might also be the society's, not just the client's.[3] Therefore, this culture says,

---

[2] Louise P. Shoemaker, "Group Work in Public Welfare," *Social Work Practice* (New York: Columbia University Press, 1967), p. 126.

[3] For further discussions related to differences in perceptions of illness and helping, see: George H. Wolkon and Arden Melzer, "Disease or Deviance: Effects on the Treatment Continuum" in *Perspectives on Deviance: Theories, Concepts and Research Findings*, Mark Lefton, James K. Skipper, and Charles H. McCaghy, eds. (New York: Appleton-Century-Crofts, 1968).

changes need to be made not only in the client's behavior but in society as well. Mediating and unifying both cultures, at least for social group workers, has been the accepted social action role. Whether the problem is the individual or society, whether in community or hospital, we have understood the need to make the environment a therapeutic one if help was to be maximized. Some of the implications were seen by Grace Coyle in 1935 when she wrote:

> In a day of individualism, it is easy enough to concentrate upon the individual and believe that his social inadequacies are due to his own maladjustment and not his environment. The typically individualistic bias of all professional workers further strengthens this natural trend so characteristic of middle class America. It is therefore not surprising if the social worker in spite of his consistent and continuous contact with the results of our social disorganization does not always take hold of his opportunities, draw conclusions in social terms from his personal observations and throw himself into one or another movements for fundamental reorganization.[4]

Our students must also be able to view some of these "new" developments in their historical perspective.

In summary, it appears that workers and students are more able to define their tasks; they are willing and able to move into agencies where the group will be used to help. Group workers are moving into child welfare, schools, public assistance, legal aid offices, and hospitals because the tasks are more clearly defined. There is growing clarity in these settings as to the goals for working with groups and the role of the worker.

So what is new in group work? What are the "new settings"? More work with adults, increased assignments in neglected agencies, concentration on the poor, assignments as supervisors and managers, emphasis on community action groups, work with individual families, short-term or crises groups, clarity of goals in work with groups, and, finally, the utilization of training centers which may open up entirely new ways of training. That is what the Cleveland area seems to be like.

What's brand new? Very little. The "field" is the same, the forces move forward, retreat, hold, and push forward again. No doubt all the things mentioned have some roots and counterpart in the history of group work, although it is what we are doing right now that counts, for as Santayana observed, "Those who cannot remember the past, are condemned to repeat it."[5]

---

[4] Ralph E. and Muriel W. Pumphrey, *The Heritage of American Social Work* (New York: Columbia University Press, 1961), p. 431.

[5] George Santayana, *Life of Reason*, revised edition (New York: Charles Scribner's Sons, 1954).

RGENCY—SCHOOL COMMUNICATION: THE INFLUENCE OF CHANGING PATTERNS OF EDUCATION

HOWARD W. BORSUK

CHANGE, one might even say drastic change, has always been a condition of life for social work education. In spite of the wear and tear on the psyches of social work educators, it seems to me that this is essentially a happy state of affairs. It is a well-worn cliché that we live, in an era of constant and accelerating social change. It is not equally evident that social work education has demonstrated the flexibility to meet the demands that these changes imply. However, new patterns of thinking about social work education are emerging. It is my purpose to describe one such pattern and to reflect on its impact on the agencies involved and their reciprocal influence on the school. I should state at the outset that the foregoing represents the product of collective effort on the part of the faculty of our school and that, in a large sense, whatever virtues are to be attributed to it belong to the faculty as a whole.

Interest in innovation in field teaching and learning at the University of Louisville Kent School of Social Work goes back to 1962, when the school undertook a major curriculum reorganization. The initial reorganization was focused on classroom teaching, but it quickly became apparent that in order to achieve our newly stated objectives, we would have to be equally concerned with field instruction. The 1962 *Curriculum Policy Statement* of the Council on Social Work Education, the

HOWARD W. BORSUK *is assistant dean at the Raymond A. Kent School of Social Work of the University of Louisville. This paper was originally presented at the Council on Social Work Education Sixteenth Annual Program Meeting in Minneapolis, Minnesota, in January, 1968.*

numerous innovative approaches and curriculum designs among schools, the constant addition of new knowledge, and the various attempts to meet the critical manpower shortage were all stimulants to our faculty in this process of change. Substantial support from the National Institute of Mental Health, the Children's Bureau, and the Vocational Rehabilitation Administration made it possible for us to expand our faculty-directed field instruction program. Our first major innovations in field instruction were in the Appalachian area of eastern Kentucky and were made possible by a grant from the Children's Bureau.

For the past two-and-a-half years we have been exploring more systematically an educational design which we feel holds exciting promise for the future. We have been stimulated by the pioneering work of the Tulane University School of Social Work, by the work of other schools of social work with whom we met in 1965, 1966, and 1967 under the auspices of the Council on Social Work Education, and by the theoretical design developed by Dr. Mildred Sikkema in connection with the Council on Social Work Education's project in field instruction.

RATIONALE

Our rationale for embarking upon this innovation came from our deep concern about the necessity to recast our objectives in light of present demands and future expectations of the field of social work practice. We are equally committed to the obligation to provide for society's deprived and incapacitated members and to a sense of social responsibility that finds expression in the profession's role in dealing with social problems and in encouraging and implementing social change. Most of us believe our profession cannot justify its existence by merely providing residual assistance to individuals, groups, and communities having problems in social functioning. We must also take leadership in identifying the social forces and structural components in our society which either enhance or hinder the effective social functioning of individuals, groups, and communities, and must suggest, devise, and implement methods of basic change in society. We feel that it is essential that educational opportunities in field instruction reflect this dual commitment to social responsibility.

We are equally concerned with the questions being raised about the compartmentalization of traditional methods of social work practice. The War on Poverty, the 1962 Social Security Amendments, the civil rights movement, Medicare, the comprehensive mental health center development, and the movement toward a guaranteed annual income are illustrations of the broad changes occurring in social welfare in our society. We have become increasingly dissatisfied with the type of field instruction which is narrowly conceived, focused on only one strategy of intervention, and bound within the confines of one agency. We feel that the future demands of our profession will call for workers with breadth and diversity, with ability to function with a variety of techniques of intervention in a variety of service settings. We feel that field instruction must reflect these considerations in the way it attempts to structure learning opportunities.

SOCIAL RESPONSIBILITY OF PROFESSION

As we attempted to restructure field instruction in line with the new professional demands, it became necessary for us to redefine the central concept of social responsibility in the social work profession. In a definition of social responsibility, three mutually interactive but analytically separate elements need to be considered: (1) the development of social work and its general area of concern; (2) the nature and obligation of a professional discipline; and (3) the more specific goals and purposes of social work as a profession.

In considering the development of social work, it is necessary to begin with a basic organizing value. Those civilizations heavily influenced by the Judeo-Christian tradition have always held that society has the obligation to provide in some way for its deprived and incapacitated members. This core value, in the historical process, has had many different expressions and has been implemented in varying degrees of strength and in a multiplicity of approaches. Social work is an element in the total network of professions, all of which may be regarded as institutional responses to recognized social need, inextricably bound to the ongoing positive welfare of society. This development has invariably involved a reciprocal process between the profession concerned and society at large, to the accompaniment of a fair degree of social consensus and sanction.

The interpretation and implementation of society's responsibility for its deprived and incapacitated members has taken many directions and achieved considerable sophistication. Social work is a direct response to the social need to discharge this obligation effectively and systematically. It has elaborated this value to mean commitment to the worth and dignity of the human person and his consequent right to share in the fruits of our society. In the Council on Social Work Education's *Curriculum Policy Statement*, the function and purpose of social work have been broadened to include concern "with the restoration, maintenance, and enhancement of social functioning. Social work contributes, with other professions and disciplines, to the prevention, treatment, and control of problems in social functioning of individuals, groups, and communities."[1]

Social responsibility in its application to social work is, in essence,

[1] *Curriculum Policy Statement* (New York: Council on Social Work Education, 1962).

the obligation to identify the social forces and structural components in our society which either enhance or hinder the effective social functioning of individuals, groups, and communities; to suggest, devise, and implement methods of amelioration or basic change within the context of need; to utilize and strengthen existing positive social forces and institutions, and to do so within a system of social sanction and professional ethical standards, accountability, and structure created by society for these purposes. It is also important to note that the identification of the above factors includes the obligation to draw society's attention to them and to help individuals, communities, and society as a whole become more conscious of their significance; in essence, to stimulate a social consciousness in regard to these factors that makes possible conscious, rational decisions relevant to the problems presented and commensurate with the state of available knowledge. The profession of social work addresses itself not just to the problems of the deprived and incapacitated, which have been its historical concerns, but to the concerns of a total population.

PLAN FOR REORGANIZING FIELD INSTRUCTION

In order to better equip students to meet the new demands of the profession as we interpret them, it became necessary to reorganize field instruction and to provide students with equal opportunities in field instruction. Learning opportunities on a carefully planned basis are provided for the first-year students to observe, participate in, and acquire beginning skills in community, group, and one-to-one relationships. Students are helped to use themselves creatively in drawing from a wide range of social work helping methods as these methods seem appropriate to a given situation. This will, we expect, make the students aware of the many potentials of social work intervention skills and help them relate to the total profession rather than to a segment of it.

The commitment to provide all students with equal opportunities involves provision of a variety of learning experiences that offer different perspectives on a given helping situation and on related social work roles. The school is in the process of building into the learning experiences of the first-year students not only situations involving the use of different methods of social work intervention at the beginning level, but also opportunities to observe and become familiar with the processes of policy formation, planning, and administration in social welfare.

Field instruction in social work hitherto has been dependent on the agency supervisor as a teacher. While this procedure may be well-suited to the initiation of the beginning worker into agency function and procedures, it is not as well-suited to the development of perspective on a given problem and exploration of all the possible helping strategies because of limits imposed by the structure and procedures of a given agency. The new field instruction plan emphasizes the educational focus and seeks to reduce dependence on the apprenticeship model as a vehicle of learning. The re-introduction of educational focus in field instruction means that the school assumes the major responsibility for field instruction by providing school-based instructors and close links between field and classroom curricula. Students are encouraged to assume greater responsibility for independent learning and learning through association with their peers. It is hoped that the wide range of learning opportunities will enable students to engage in productive and creative assessment of their helping roles and functions.

ELEMENTS OF THE NEW PLAN

A major task in the implementation of the new plan involves the recasting of the educational objectives of field instruction and the systematic development of appropriate curriculum content to include an overview of society, the nature and functions of social institutions, the different organization of welfare functions, and the various kinds of social work professional roles. These are viewed within a value framework, grouped under several organizing concepts, and divided into specific time periods. Curriculum innovations are extended to encompass classroom instruction as well so that field and class provide a common framework for total learning.

All first-year students are grouped into sections of 12, each with a separate field instructor. All sections are based at and operated from the school. The field instructor for each section assumes the major responsibility for planning and developing appropriate learning experiences, for gearing the section to the overall curriculum plan, and for maintaining continuity and progression in student learning. Although a section consists of 12 students, they do not always operate as a 12-member group. Depending upon a given situation and the anticipated learning potentials, students may operate in smaller sub-sections of varying sizes or in combination with other sections. Reasons for setting the section size at 12 include: the flexibility for working in groups of differing size; manageability from the point of view of the instructor; and optimum opportunity for communication between section members. Each section meets as a whole at least once a week to plan, assess, and evaluate learning experiences in the light of the stated curriculum objectives. It is important to note that, although these innovations pertain at this time only to the first year, we are keenly aware of the impact on our second-year program and are preparing to examine these implications.

THE SOCIAL PROBLEM FOCUS OF THE FIELD INSTRUCTION SECTIONS

The objectives of the field instruction sections are not separate from, but part of, the total educational program of the school. The first-year

Kent School student is expected to realize and incorporate these objectives, which include the ability to observe critically and to comprehend social welfare institutions and their organization, and the acquisition of beginning professional values and skills relevant to the social welfare needs and problems. Membership in a field instruction section enables the student to realize these objectives by focusing his learning on a given social problem area. It is not intended that he gain exclusive expertise in a problem area but that he use it as an example of the incidence of need or problem in a community and of the existing coping mechanisms and relevant social work professional roles.

There are several pragmatic reasons that have commended the social problem focus to the field instruction sections. The foremost is that, in most communities, welfare functions are organized around social problems such as mental health, child welfare, poverty, and crime. The social problem focus also facilitates study and examination of the corresponding coping mechanisms from a micro as well as a macro point of view in terms of their adequacies and inadequacies, the value system that they reflect, and the nature of social work response—current as well as projected.

The term "social problem" is open to several interpretations. In a narrow sense, it "denotes a condition affecting a significant number of people in ways considered undesirable, about which it is felt something can be done through collective social action."[2] Social problem is also described as a condition seen by a considerable number of persons as a deviation from the norm, which they cherish. As Merton puts it, "The same social structure and culture that, in the main, make for conforming and organized behavior also generate tendencies toward distinctive kinds of deviant behavior and potentials of social disorganization. In this sense, the problems current in a society register the social costs of a particular organization of social life. . . . It follows also that, to a substantial extent, social problems are the unwilled, largely indirect, and often unanticipated consequences of institutionalized patterns of a social behavior."[3] Implicit in these definitions is the dominant role that values play in determining what is and what is not an undesirable condition and also in what is sanctioned and provided as an appropriate coping mechanism. When viewed narrowly, the above definitions of social problem assign a role to the profession of social work of assisting individuals, groups, and communities who are having problems in their social functioning and in adjusting to the *status quo*. However, Merton's view also implies alteration in the social structure as well.

Kent School approaches the concept of social problem in broad terms,

---

[2] Paul B. Horton and Gerald R. Leslie, *The Sociology of Social Problems*, Third edition, 1965.

[3] Robert K. Merton and Robert A. Nisbet, *Contemporary Social Problems*, Second edition, 1966.

as part of a large constellation of need conditions, some of which, when filtered through the existing dominant value screen are recognized as social problems warranting community attention and action through appropriately sanctioned welfare structures. In addition, the school seeks to alert the student to those significant sections of need conditions that escape the attention of the community because of the particular community value pattern, and to those need conditions that have attracted some community recognition for which the institutional response is either inappropriate or inadequate. In short, the students are encouraged to inquire into and explore the nature of the existing welfare organization relative to a given social problem, to look further for clues to the identification and definition of that social problem, to seek the corresponding value constellation, and, where appropriate, to explore ways and means of bringing to bear on the problem the influence of professional social work values.

CURRICULUM

Although curriculum planning for classroom instruction existed from the early days of social work education, there is little evidence of similar activity in regard to field instruction. Traditionally, objectives and content in field instruction were seen largely in experiential terms, which, in turn, were substantially left to the determination of the agency supervisor. In line with the revised structuring of field teaching, the Kent School decided to state its field instruction objectives in explicit terms and to translate these objectives into identifiable components of specific content, divided into viable time periods. At this time this process is far from complete, and the field instruction faculty is continuing its work with the dual goal of achieving greater clarity in the definition of objectives and content and of bringing a greater unity between classroom and field instruction.

EVALUATION

The Kent School's innovations in field instruction have been introduced into the curriculum in gradual stages and have been constantly subjected by the faculty to close scrutiny and examination. There is continued awareness of the need to understand more fully the nature of these innovations and to find ways to incorporate them systematically into the total curriculum.

Evaluation in field instruction is seen primarily as a knowledge-building process. One member of the research faculty assists the field instructors in the evaluation of field instruction. At this stage, the role of evaluation is visualized as inculcating in the faculty a spirit of inquiry, rather than setting up experiments to test specific hypotheses or developing exact measuring devices. As mentioned earlier, our most pressing need is to understand the various implications of our innovations in field instruction and their impact on the student learning process. To achieve the goal of equal learning opportunities for all students, all the field instruction sections must have basic agreement on common goals and objectives and on specific content and procedures. We need to know more about student reaction and response to these field instruction opportunities and about use of student reactions to further clarify and revise field instruction procedures. This points toward the identification and development of objective indices of student progress in field instruction.

Weekly meetings of field instruction faculty have provided valuable feedback and sharing of information leading to a better understanding between field instruction sections and have contributed to assessment of accomplishments in each individual section. Weekly logs kept by field instructors, student reports of their weekly section meetings, and individual student reactions gathered at different periods of time are illustrative of the data collected so far.

AGENCY-SCHOOL RELATIONSHIPS

A large part of the stimulus for the above changes came from the field. Agency executives, in an informal survey, indicated to us that they are looking almost desperately for social workers with the kind of broad educational experience described here. Agencies have been hampered in providing new services and programs and in developing new methods of helping by lack of professional personnel equipped to respond to the challenges involved. This is not a universal phenomenon, however, for some agencies continue to function along traditional lines and are satisfied with a relatively narrow focus. Yet this is distinctly a minority view and the winds of change blow strong. In this connection, the school has crucial responsibility to set up a structure for an on-going dialogue for communication of the rationale and the content of change. There are many avenues for doing this. It may be done, as we have done in our school, by setting up periodic seminars for agency executives and annual retreats for agency-and school-based field instructors, by creating a variety of special committees composed of a mix of faculty and agency field instructors, and by frequent informal contact between field section instructors and executives and staffs of participating agencies.

We have already seen some of the results of this process of improved communication; for example, the greater readiness to use groups in traditional casework agencies, the emerging interest in community and the desire to become involved in effecting community change, the reaching out to hitherto untouched clients and, in the process, trying out new approaches in help. Accompanying these changes is a renewed interest in studying the total environment with a view to effecting pertinent alterations in the service patterns and a connected interest in the literature of social sciences. Of significant importance to the field work section plan is the increasing number of social agencies that can be used for educational experiences. In addition, with school-directed field curriculum and school-based field instructors, we are no longer confined to agencies that meet a designated standard of service, particularly in reference to the employment of skilled professional social work staff. Such agencies, through experience with students, move to upgrade their services and to develop new patterns of thought and program. This description only hints at the potentials for development of breadth and flexibility in field instruction, in social work education, and in agency practice that can result from free, creative, and reciprocal communication between agency and school.

A SOCIAL SERVICES CENTER FOR A MULTI-PROBLEM COMMUNITY

DONALD BRIELAND

FOLLOWING its establishment in Hyde Park, the University of Chicago watched the community gradually decay. After some time, it was motivated to take a leading role in rehabilitating the neighborhood. The University is now developing its South Campus in Woodlawn, another neighborhood with very serious social problems. With the recent purchase of additional land in Woodlawn, the University will find itself even more involved in this community.

Woodlawn is composed of 560 acres and is irregularly shaped, averaging about seven blocks by 12 blocks. In 1960, 80,000 persons were crammed into this area; today, its population is even greater. Many of its apartment houses and small hotels were built to house visitors to the Columbian Exposition in 1893. It remained a relatively stable middle-class community until some 15 years ago. Now, at least 28 percent of the housing units are classed as sub-standard.

Twenty-four percent of the residents have an annual family income under $3,000. The unemployment rate is ten percent—three times the national average. One-fourth of the population gets some type of public assistance. Over 4,000 families receive Aid to Dependent Children. Preschool children constitute 12 percent of the population. Last year's public school enrollments suggest that at least 98.5 percent of the population is Negro. This fall, absenteeism from school was high because of the required payment of tribute money for safe conduct exacted by gang members from some of the children. Most of the cases reported by Billings Hospital, under the provisions of the Child Abuse Law, are

DONALD BRIELAND is associate dean at the School of Social Service Administration, University of Chicago, Chicago, Illinois. This paper was presented at the Council on Social Work Education Fifteenth Annual Program Meeting in Salt Lake City, Utah, January, 1967. This paper appeared in the Social Work Education Reporter, Vol. 15, No. 3 (September, 1967), pp. 30 ff.

victims of long-term neglect and parental incapacity rather than of acute violence.

Woodlawn provides an illustration of the effects of poverty. As described by a member of the Oberlin College faculty:

> Poverty produces the sense of being shaped by forces beyond one's understanding and control, which renders the self insecure in all its aspects— physical well-being, personal relationships, moral and intellectual beliefs. Finally, and as a result of these conditions, poverty is a feeling of personal unimportance. The conviction that *self* is worthless is what distinguishes modern poverty from the "honest poor" of old or the ascetics of religious tradition.[1]

UNIVERSITY INTEREST IN WOODLAWN

Why is the University involved with Woodlawn? The University is not in the welfare business, but it must be concerned with making its campus and the neighborhoods in which most of its employees live as wholesome and as safe as possible. Through its Urban Studies Center, its hospitals, and its School of Social Service Administration, the university has the know-how to be helpful with major social problems. It must take an active part in efforts to combat poverty, delinquency, and unrest. Bringing social agencies together to provide further research and better service is one way to do this.

George Beadle, president of the University, in a letter to Robert Weaver, [former] secretary of the U.S. Department of Housing and Urban Development, made the following statement concerning the University's interest in Woodlawn:

> While the University's major tasks are education and research, we are necessarily concerned with the welfare of the community. We are particularly pleased when education objectives can be achieved through programs that also provide service to the community. The proposed Social Services Center will achieve this combination of objectives. . . .
>
> Although it is neither possible nor appropriate for the University to operate large welfare services programs, we do know that there are important mutual benefits to be derived through cooperation with appropriate agencies operated by the State, the County, and the City, as well as private agencies.

EXPERIMENTAL CENTERS

Why is the field of social work interested in such experimental centers? The establishment of the teaching hospital under university ownership or control was one of the significant steps in the development of medical education and the encouragement of research. The concept of

---

[1] Wilson C. McWilliams, "Poverty: Public Enemy Number One," *Saturday Review*, December 10, 1966, pp. 48 ff.

62

the teaching hospital goes back a half century to Flexner's study of medical education for the Carnegie Foundation. Although the modern medical school also utilizes the community clinic as a locus for new efforts in such specialities as psychiatry and pediatrics, the teaching hospital still provides the base for professional education. The parallel in the education of teachers is the laboratory school. Innovations are often developed here and further tested in the public schools. For professional social work, the pattern has been quite different. Public and voluntary agencies have been used for field instruction and research, but schools of social work have not had a facility under their control analogous to the teaching hospital or the laboratory school. This has made it difficult for teaching faculty to continue their practice of social work and for schools to develop new directions and provide a secure base for research. John Gardner, [former] secretary of the Department of Health, Education, and Welfare, in a speech at the 1965 Annual Program Meeting of the Council on Social Work Education, discussed projected developments in schools of social work that he hoped would come about.

I suggest that we project ourselves into the future about a quarter of a century. If you are using the same crystal ball that I am, you will see the following things quite clearly.

First, the universities will have established themselves even more profoundly as important nerve centers of society. The inner city of the university will concern itself with the basic fields of science and scholarship at both undergraduate and graduate levels. And that inner city will be ringed with great and powerful professional schools which will serve as the bridge between the university and the rest of the community, between basic and applied knowledge, between the idea and its uses.

Among these professional schools, the school of social work will be one of the most important. . . .

Like all of the great professional schools of 1990, it will have extremely close ties with the basic fields of science and scholarship in the university—in this case, with the behavioral and social sciences. Indeed, it will not be ranked as a distinguished school of social work unless it is associated with an institution in which those fields are strong.

Over and above the basic research activities in the university, the school of social work will itself carry on extensive research, both basic and applied. It will conduct its own appraisal of social needs and problems. It will look into the methods by which social services are delivered as well as the institution arrangements through which the needs of people are met. . . .

In short, the great complex of gleaming buildings that make up the University Social Work Center of 1990 will have many laboratories for social research.[2]

---

[2] John W. Gardner, "Remarks by John W. Gardner," *Journal of Education for Social Work*, Vol. 2, No. 1 (Spring, 1966), pp. 6-7.

ESTABLISHING A CENTER IN WOODLAWN

Why is the School of Social Service Administration interested in a center in Woodlawn? For many years, Alton A. Linford, dean of the School of Social Service Administration, has been highlighting the need for a facility in which the school would have considerable responsibility for the programs, a facility conveniently located to the school and designed with its needs as a central concern.

The opportunity to develop such a concept was realized in 1965 when the Children's Bureau, through its Research Division, invited Dean Linford to develop a proposal to study the feasibility of a "clinical research and teaching facility," the social welfare equivalent of the teaching hospital.

In the project that resulted, the far-reaching objectives of the Children's Bureau were accepted:

1. Improve the quality of teaching.
2. Provide a setting for research and demonstration.
3. Improve the quality of public child welfare and related services.
4. Upgrade the entire field of social welfare through the demonstration of what can be done in child welfare.

In the last 14 months, a Social Services Center concept has been developed that should have a profound effect on the delivery of social services in the community in which the School of Social Service Administration is located. At the same time, it should strengthen social work education and increase the opportunities for research.

The present School of Social Service Administration building is on the edge of Woodlawn across the Midway from Billings Hospital. The proposed Social Services Center will be located on the southeast corner of the block on which the school is located, on Sixty-first Street and Ingleside Avenue. The Center will be on the campus and in the community. Both the nature of the community and its convenience to the school make Woodlawn an ideal location for the Center.

SOCIAL SERVICE CENTER PROGRAMS

It was felt essential that the Center be university owned and controlled. It was soon found that a much larger, more diversified, and more significant program could be provided if existing agencies were invited to cooperate in the Center rather than if the school tried to establish and operate an agency of its own. A significant Center program must involve the large public agencies serving children and their families. This will result in a much less selective intake policy than that of the typical teaching hospital. The Center will also concentrate on out-patient services, although cooperative agreements will also be sought eventually with in-patient facilities, especially children's institutions. While their interests in demonstration projects, training, and research have been clearly expressed, existing agencies are limited by their policies and statutory authority. Can the Center help them to operationalize this interest, and can grants and other special financial support be found to cover some of the costs of new programs? What services should be included in a Social Services Center program to strengthen family life? Except for the public schools, the Department of Public Aid, through its AFDC program, is involved with more families than any other part of the health, education, and welfare system. This program must provide a major component for the Center.

PROVISION OF DAY CARE

In a poverty area with a great need for maternal employment and a high incidence of child neglect, day care is essential. The community had attempted for several years to find a location for a large, publicly operated, day care center. Although community leaders had convinced the State Department of Children and Family Services of the need for such a center, no building in Woodlawn met the health and safety requirements for licensing. The school's study of the community indicated that at least 500 children could profit from group day care, with additional numbers needing similar foster family and after-school services. All three types are necessary to provide a comprehensive program.

A way is also needed to identify preschool children who, although from families above the public assistance level, still have serious problems that otherwise would not come to light until the child entered school. The maternal and child health centers of the Board of Health constitute an excellent case-finding resource to do this. Fortunately, the commissioner of Health has authorized development of an extensive social services program in the Woodlawn clinic.

In addition, pledges of support and cooperation have been given by the Chicago Child Care Society, a leading voluntary child welfare agency providing foster care, adoption, and day care services, and United Charities, the family service agency with a district office in Woodlawn.

A relationship has also been established with the Woodlawn Organization, the "grass roots" community action group, and the school has also been in communication with the local Urban Progress Center, the community referral resource established under the anti-poverty program.

CONSTRUCTION PLANS

Since the present programs in Woodlawn are poorly coordinated, there are many advantages in locating most of the component agencies of the Center in one building. The cost will be nearly two million dollars. The Neighborhood Facilities Program of the Department of Housing and Urban Development has approved an application from the City of Chicago for two-thirds of the construction cost. Now the University must raise the other one-third, about $700,000. At the same time, programs will be initiated with the various agencies while the building is being planned. The project staff will operate in rental space during the next two years. Only the day care center is entirely dependent upon a new building. In the fall of 1967, tooling up will begin for an education experiment in the Center. Twenty first-year students will be assigned to Center agencies. For each student, methods and field instruction under the same faculty member will be conducted in the Center so that theory and practice can be fully integrated. At the same time, a generalist approach will be utilized. As part of their professional education, students will have experience with more than one method and will follow families through various service contacts. They will also develop comprehensive service plans based on diagnoses of families served. There are many opportunities to employ group methods in agencies affiliated with the Center. The problems of families in Woodlawn also often require the use of community organization principles for their solution.

Students assigned to the Center will be representative of those admitted to the regular first-year program so that general comparisons can be made. The Center students will use the summer for an intensive placement and will complete the MSW program in six consecutive quarters.

As a result of the experience with the first pilot group, an evaluative design will be developed for use with students admitted in 1968.

ISSUES FOR POSSIBLE RESEARCH

The concept "culturally disadvantaged" lumps together children with different needs, capabilities, and behavior. The range in the AFDC group, for example, extends from children whose problems are almost entirely financial, to victims of physical abuse, to those who are seriously emotionally disturbed. In Woodlawn, the expectation is to begin by concentrating on preschool children whose family life puts them in jeopardy. A target population of the Center will be children from AFDC families who are likely to be removed from their homes because of neglect, abuse, or parental incapacity. At least 20 percent of the AFDC families fall into such an extreme group. A major challenge is to differentiate the transitory effects of environmental stress from deeper pathology.

This sort of population provides many opportunities for research. Virtually all of the previous studies involved children who had already been separated. In this instance, the mothering process can be studied at several points before separation and during the period that intensive special services are provided to try to prevent placement. Both groups can then be followed—the children who remain with their mothers and

66

those for whom placement is the plan chosen. Several methods of delivery of service to this group can also be compared. In addition, it will be possible to derive data on dependency extending over two or more generations. The concern is with both causes and strategies for service. One example is the possible priority of service for the eldest daughter in the family. If she follows the pattern of early pregnancy and dependency, does she have a prepotent influence on younger siblings? Can work with her in pre-adolescence affect the outcome for younger family members?

Another possibly profitable line of inquiry concerns the sex role concepts of mothers of children from AFDC families. One theory suggests that the mother's differing concepts of appropriate sex roles reduce the academic achievement drive of the boy and enhance it for the girl. The mother may want the boy to be pleasant and likeable but not really want him to succeed. This may stem from a desire to enhance the dominant female role.

TREATMENT STRATEGIES

What makes sense as a treatment strategy? There cannot possibly be enough child guidance resources to make a dent. School social work service provides a promising approach to some of the most serious problems. Can intervention be more successful in the preschool period through a protective program in AFDC and social services in maternal and child health?

Another important concern is to provide more continuity in social services. Clients have to tell their story a half-dozen times to get service from six different agencies. At present, a family known to one agency may be caught up in a net so that it is hampered in getting help from other agencies. At the same time, families may be motivated to play one agency off against another. One research proposal involves use of modern data processing to study the utilization of social services by Woodlawn residents. This would represent a modern version of the Social Services Exchange and provide substantial amounts of information on very short notice.

Along with training and research, the Center will be especially interested in the young child and the opportunities that he provides for preventive intervention; it will be interested in improving the quality of service; and it will be concerned with the most effective coordination of community efforts.

PART III
TEACHING AND LEARNING
IN THE FIELD

SELECTED FEATURES OF PROFESSIONAL FIELD INSTRUCTION

SAMUEL FINESTONE

FIELD INSTRUCTION conceived as part of professional education for social work emphasizes intellectual and emotional learning and the acquisition of attitudes and skills. Without implying the lesser importance of other aspects, four selected features of field instruction will be discussed here. Professional field instruction is assumed to be characterized by:

1. A method of teaching that stresses learning of generalizations drawn from specific, related experiences: in a word, conceptual learning. Conceptual learning is contrasted with a style of teaching that stresses learning of isolated bits of knowledge and skill, using the field supervisor as master model and the student as apprentice.

2. A range of content that reflects the total social work curriculum, and not the understanding and mastery of a specific social work method alone.

3. Attention not only to what is currently known and practiced, but also to the preparation of students for changes in the knowledge base, organization of services, and methods of practice of social work. Preparing students for change is contrasted to an apprentice style of teaching and learning that takes the current state of social work knowledge and practice as fixed.

4. Provision not only for reflection of the class curriculum but also for feedback and impact on the class curriculum.

To meet these criteria for professional field instruction, a working

SAMUEL FINESTONE *is assistant dean of the Columbia University School of Social Work and chairman of the CSWE Commission on Educational Research. This paper is a slightly revised version of a presentation given at the Annual Field Work Institute, University of Connecticut School of Social Work, Hartford, Connecticut, April, 1967, and was published in the* Journal of Education for Social Work, *Vol. 3, No. 2 (Fall, 1967), pp. 14-26.*

partnership of class and field faculty is necessary. Conceptual learning in the field will not take place until class and field teachers identify important concepts and generalizations, share them, and share experiences in the methods through which they may be taught and learned. The total class curriculum will not be reflected in the field until channels and devices are strengthened or invented for class-field communication. An orientation to change is not educationally transmissible unless both class and field instructors are at least receptive to, if not actively involved in, change efforts. Finally, impact of field developments on class curriculum depends upon the activity, scholarly reflection, and research of field instructors; on channels for communication of field to class; and on the interest of faculty instructors in such communication.

All these considerations, taken together, support the notion of a class-field partnership in an educational enterprise with mutual feedback of new developments contributing a dynamic for change.

THE NATURE AND ART
OF CONCEPTUAL TEACHING IN THE FIELD

Conceptual teaching may be defined most broadly as the art of stimulating generalized and generalizable learning. Conceptual teaching is described as an *art*, because it requires imaginative selectivity, creativity, and skill on the part of the field instructor. *Generalized* learning connotes the understanding of unifying concepts, propositions, and principles which connect a mass of details in an economical way. *Generalizable* learning signifies the kind of learning that enables students to apply the generalized results to new experiences. Conceptual learning is the crystallization of experience; the teacher's art is the practice of assisting the student to achieve this crystallization.

Conceptual teaching focuses consciously and specifically on the intellectual underpinnings of practice. The aim of such teaching is not only, or not so much, to guide or modify the student's work with a particular situation, but to gain understanding of the general conceptual elements involved. The aim is not service *per se,* although this must and will take place, but the generalized learning which can be distilled out of the experience of giving service. The aim is not to have the student learn a case, but to learn from it. The field instructor, selecting and preparing for assignment of a case to a student, asks himself not only "What does the case need?" but "What can the student learn from this case? What concepts, propositions, and principles are involved; How are these related to those that the student is learning from class and reading?"

It may be useful at this point to define the terms that describe basic elements in conceptualization: concept, proposition, principle, and theory. Difficulty occurs because these terms are used in various ways. Even at the risk of arbitrariness, it seems important to attempt to arrive at some common understanding in order to facilitate communication. A concept is a word or phrase that we use inside our heads, or in communicating to others, to express in a summarized way a property or properties considered to be common to a group of entities. The most important part of this definition is the idea that a concept is a name for what is considered to be common to a group of things.

Concepts may be relatively simple or complex. "Chair" is a name for a group of objects that have as their common characteristic an arrangement of physical materials to accommodate a certain portion of the human anatomy in a sitting position. This simple example suggests that most, if not all, words are concepts. Further, simple concepts are part of larger classes of ideas of greater and greater abstraction. Thus, "chair" may be subsumed under the larger term "furniture" when concern is no longer with the sitting use of a chair, but rather with more general aspects, which it shares with other kinds of furniture. And "furniture" may be subsumed under "household equipment," or, going even further up the ladder of abstraction, under "technological features of a culture." This is a complex concept which might be of use to a cultural anthropologist but not to a carpenter, for whom "chair" is the more relevant concept.

But what about concepts used in social work? Most of them are very complex since they summarize in one term a great many properties. The concept "delinquency" refers to certain kinds of behavior that conflict with laws. It is part of a larger class of behavior that may be called "deviant behavior," a term which includes mental illness and other norm-violating behavior. The concept "resistance" is one of a class of behaviors manifested by clients in treatment through different types of avoidance of painful or conflictual material. "Social class" is a concept referring to the location in society of an individual or group on a low to high scale based on such factors as income, education, and employment. "Clarification" is a term used to describe a class of behavior used by social workers in their attempts to help clients. In all of these oversimplified examples, the interest is not in an individual instance, but that which expresses what is common to a *number* of instances.

Concepts can be distinguished from propositions and principles, both of which utilize concepts. Propositions are statements about the way phenomena, summed up in the form of concepts, are related to each other. Thus it is possible to say that in the stress of acute illness, people are likely to have a period in which they return to earlier, regressive, dependent behavior, but that this tendency will vary with a number of personal and social factors. Now there are a number of *concepts* in this statement, or proposition. The concepts are very broadly and imprecisely expressed, but the point is that a statement is being made, or a proposition formulated, in which various concepts are related to each other as a shorthand way of expressing a generalization about real relationships. Concepts become increasingly meaningful when their relationships to other concepts are elaborated in propositions or principles.

Whether or not a proposition is true is a different matter. It may be assumed as true on the basis of previous experience without formal proof; or it may be stated as true on the basis of formal proof or research; or it may be put in the form of a hypothesis to be tested. So propositions may be assumptions, or statements based on formal proof, or hypotheses to be tested.

Like propositions, principles also deal with relationships between concepts; but they are action-oriented rather than description- or existence-oriented. Propositions describe existing relationships (descriptive); principles give rules for action (prescriptive). To follow up on the proposition about the relationship between stress, acute illness, regressive action, and contingent psycho-social factors—what social work principles can be derived from this proposition, what rules for action? Of course, there would not be any simple or unequivocal guides, since the nature of the phenomena dealt with does not permit this. But a principle might go something like this: social workers should accept an initial period of dependent, regressive behavior on the part of patients suffering from acute and dangerous illness in order to facilitate effective use of medical treatment and later positive outcome. This is an imprecise statement, yet it serves to illustrate the difference between a proposition and a principle.

The fourth and broadest term is "theory." "Theory" generally means an interrelated set of propositions or principles. Behavioral theory would then refer to related propositions about behavior; practice theory would refer to related principles of practice, which in turn are based on propositions about behavior.

Perhaps this part of the discussion can be summarized with an analogy, which, like other analogies, has both usefulness and dangers. Concepts are like words; propositions or principles are like sentences; and theories are like paragraphs. The analogy is that both concepts and words are the elements of larger statements. Both propositions and principles on the one hand, and sentences on the other, are statements that relate different elements to each other. Finally, both theories and paragraphs are made up of a series of interrelated statements.

The Method of Conceptual Teaching

So much, then, for what is meant by conceptual teaching. The next task is to make some suggestions as to how it is done.[1] There are some pre-conditions for conceptual teaching. The first is that the field in-

---

[1] Many of the ideas in this section are found in Jeanette Regensburg, "Report of Exploratory Project in Field Instruction," *Field Instruction in Graduate Social Work Education: Old Problems and New Proposals* (New York: Council on Social Work Education, 1966).

structor is clear about selected concepts and generalizations that are to be taught and that these concepts and generalizations are related to those which underlie class content. If there is this clarity, if there is this sense of a curriculum of conceptual content, then the field instructor will be quick to see, or to create, opportunities to stimulate conceptual learning. Another requirement is that the field instructor have time to analyze cases and student recording: to think out what conceptual content is involved and how the student conference can be used for conceptual learning. It is assumed that the field instructor thinks of himself as an educator and that the structuring of his role and his status encourages this kind of perception.

Conceptual teaching may be inductive or deductive in method. In inductive teaching, the direction is from a set of particulars to a general concept or statement. The point is to help the student to identify, or to identify for him, what can be found in common among a group of instances of client characteristics, or behavior, or his own behavior in attempting to help clients. "Client systems" might be a better term to reflect the fact that the student may be dealing with an individual personality system, a family system, a group system, a neighborhood system, an agency system, etc.[2] The basic teaching question is, "What do we see in common among these various instances, and what do we call it?" Thus, even within a single case, the student may look at various bits of behavior manifested by a client and see that they all express, in various forms, a common theme; for example, a desire for assurance or permission. Or, in working with a group, a variety of behaviors of members may be linked under the common concept of "scapegoating." Or, in relating to an institutional system, the concept of "power structure" may emerge from instances of how and where decisions are made. These are examples of induction of concepts, but the same approach would apply to propositions about behavior or treatment principles.

Even more than with a single case or group, comparisons among a number of cases or groups lend themselves to conceptual teaching or learning. Cross-comparisons of similar elements in a number of situations and the identification and naming of what is held in common (the concept, proposition, or principle), is at the heart of conceptual learning.

In deductive teaching, the direction is from a generalization to particulars. The strategic question is, "Given a concept, proposition, or principles, what example can be given?" Thus the field instructor may say, "There is a generalization to the effect that different members in a group may assume expressive leadership and task leadership roles. What are examples of the division of leadership roles?"

---

[2] An early discussion of the application of Parsonian "System Theory" to social casework is given in Werner A. Lutz, "Concepts and Principles Underlying Social Work Practice" (New York: National Association of Social Workers, 1956).

In either inductive or deductive teaching, the field instructor may be more or less active. The student may spontaneously search for the common element in a series of instances, or search for examples of a generalization. The field instructor may stimulate this kind of thinking by asking questions. Finally, the field instructor may be maximally active by formulating the generalization from particulars (induction) or by giving specific illustrations of general principles (deduction). The presentation of inductive and deductive approaches appears to make too sharp a distinction between them. Often, discussion of the relationship between the particular and the general combines, or moves back and forth between, inductive and deductive approaches.

Conceptual teaching has been described as an intellectual art. So it is, because there are choices to be made as to what generalizations to emphasize, what levels of complexity to aim at, whether to emphasize inductive or deductive approaches, and how much instructor activity to stimulate. The rules for making these decisions are not clear cut and the decisions cannot be programmed. It is suggested that a number of factors enter into these decisions. As far as the selection of conceptual elements is concerned, it would seem wise to look for the spots where the student's experiences in class and field intersect. This involves knowing what the student is learning in his classes as well as analyzing the student's field experiences from the point of view of conceptual learning opportunities.

The choice of inductive or deductive approaches might well be influenced by the learning style of the student. Some students need to have experiences before they can comprehend generalizations; they are doers and learn best inductively. Other students ask for propositions and principles in advance of experience and learn best deductively. So the teaching approach of the field instructor may be flexibly adjusted to the learning style of the student; even though the objective of conceptualized knowledge is the same.

The field instructor's ability to grasp common elements in a mass of particulars and to see specific and vivid illustrations of generalizations is basic. These are the necessary qualities of the instructor in either the class or field setting, which, together with sensitivity to the learning needs and style of students, are among the central characteristics of professional education for social work.

CONCEPTUALIZED CONTENT IN FIELD TEACHING

It is generally agreed that academic and practice experiences should be related to each other for sound teaching and effective learning. It is also agreed that the class-field educational relationship should extend beyond the selected content of the social work method to the content of the total curriculum. The rationale for this agreement is not difficult to state: intellectual and emotional understanding of class content is more likely to take place if it is exemplified, reinforced, extended, and even challenged in the context of field experience.

In spite of this agreement, there appear to be discrepancies between educational intentions for integrated class-field content and achievement of this end. The discrepancies exist in all schools of social work to a greater or lesser degree and, therefore, warrant attention.

It may be useful to identify the reasons for these discrepancies. It takes considerable effort, time, and vision to construct devices for interchange between class and field instructors so that the current class content is known to all and the conceptual elements identified. Since social work knowledge is not fixed, but developing both in the class and in the field, devices for interchange must be continuing ones. Also, there is a turnover of teaching personnel in class and field, particularly in the latter, and this complicates communication. Even beyond these difficulties, there is the problem of the time sequence of content in class and field. The class instructor can logically order the content he teaches to observe the principles of continuity and progression from simpler to more complex. This is difficult for the field instructor since the learning experiences of the student cannot all be arranged by plan.

The difficulties in coordinating class-field instruction have led some schools of social work to experiment with new models of field instruction in which field experiences are devised as a laboratory extension of class instruction. These approaches seem to sidestep the problems of integrating class and field content usually found when students are placed in a single agency with early and continuing service assignments. However, other problems may arise when case assignments are delayed, when students rotate in a number of agencies, and when other changes are made in the usual arrangement for field instruction. This paper assumes the usual field instruction arrangement which, in spite of difficulties, has potentialities for integrating class-field content. These potentialities can be seen if specific areas of curriculum content are discussed, particularly areas other than social work method and human behavior, in order to emphasize the total range of curriculum content. The first area to be so considered is that of social policy and social service content in field teaching.

SOCIAL POLICY AND SOCIAL SERVICES CONTENT IN FIELD TEACHING

Is there a connection between the policies, procedures, and structure which shape agency activity and the content of social policy and social services courses? If so, how can the relevant content in the field be identified? How can this content be used to construct field learning experiences for students which will reinforce, or concretize, or extend, class teaching?

The underlying conception of social policy-social service content is basic to these questions. If social policy is viewed narrowly as that which has to do with social welfare legislation, then some potential for field teaching can be seen, even though it is limited. But in a broad sense, every agency makes social policy, and every agency is affected by it. Social policy is the making of decisions among alternative goals and the means of achieving these goals. The decisions are based on values related to the welfare of people; to the prime social work value which may be expressed as individual fulfillment in social living. This is, one is forced to acknowledge reluctantly, an unrealistic and idealistic statement. In the real world other considerations enter into the making of decisions: the availability of resources; the sanction of the community; and the realities of power distribution. Social workers are rarely faced with a choice between pure good and pure evil: more often they are faced with a choice between or among competing values. Value choices most often involve compromises. There are alternative means of achieving values that require evaluation as well. Nevertheless, every agency is faced with choices, even if within limits, and these choices are the stuff of social policy. What is to be demonstrated is that social policy questions are interwoven inextricably with all social work practice: social workers are all, actively or passively, in the business of social policy.

Social agency policies and procedures are the result of decisions. Some of these decisions are consciously and explicitly made, others are implicit and not made with full consciousness. These decisions have consequences which are either intended or unintended. The consequences affect the way the agency serves its own clientele, and they affect the social meeting of need in the community at large. These agency decisions and consequences bear examination, and this examination is, or should be, part of course content. As a corollary point, it follows that the ability to examine the value and practical base of decisions on agency policy, and the anticipated and unanticipated consequences of such decisions, is a suitable objective for student learning.

Agencies are related to and affected by larger systems: the social welfare network of agencies with which they interact as well as the general community systems—legislative, political, economic, and so on. Agency practice and service is inevitably affected by the structure and policies of these larger systems. Here too, there is much to be aware of, to analyze, to adapt to, and perhaps to participate in changing. Both within the agency system and within its inter-system relationships, there are policies and structures to understand and to evaluate in preparation for future professional responsibilities: these responsibilities may lie in the area of change. Students should indeed learn to identify with, and accommodate to, an agency; but they should also learn to evaluate its policy and structure as well as to evaluate the policy and structure of the larger system with which it is engaged.

With these broad considerations sketched, some field learning experiences of particular relevance to the understanding of both social policy and social service content, and to skills and attitudes involved in its examination by students, may be outlined.

The beginning of a student's placement is usually marked by planned orientation. It would seem that a dynamic history of the agency, presented as part of this orientation, has rich learning content. Embedded in the origin and development of the agency are a series of significant decisions. How did the agency originally define the problems that needed attention, and how did these definitions change? What were its objectives—that is, what were the objectives of its activity? What kinds of outcomes did it originally, and later, conceive as desirable? How did it originally, and later, define its clientele and its staff? Where did it originally, and later, derive its support and sanction? What kinds of program and services were developed?

The admission policies and procedures of an agency set down decisions about who shall and who shall not be served. Every admission policy is also an exclusion policy. There are important policy decisions involved that might well be examined rather than taken for granted. The full implications of the question "Whom does the agency serve?" cannot be explored unless there is some comparison of the characteristics of the population served by the agency with the characteristics of the general population. Within the admission policies, there are criteria for eligibility or accessibilty that similarly merit examination, since they may have consequences that were not originally intended. The educational question is whether, and how, field work students should be exposed to this kind of examination of agency admission policies, both for the knowledge involved and for the development of an attitude of critical inquiry considered part of professional competence.

So far, aspects of the agency as a whole have been discussed as sources for social policy learning. But there are also opportunities within the student's direct service assignments for such learning. At least, there are such opportunities if the proposition is accepted that individuals, families, and groups are most fully understood and helped in the context of their connections with the larger social structure and the social provisions and deprivations of opportunity and resources. In this sense, each case or group is a source of knowledge of social needs and the adequacy of social resources to meet these needs. The professional vision of students may be broadened if cases are considered not only in the framework of individual need but also in the framework of implied social needs and required social action.

The discussion leads to the relation between the agency and the larger social welfare and community network with which it interacts. As the agency attempts to help clients relate to other agencies or to the general community, there appear difficulties in coordination, deficits in resources. Surely every agency can give examples. Perhaps a smaller number of agencies can also provide examples of systematic efforts to improve the situation through various kinds of study and action channels. If so, students' experiences are ready-made for identification of social policy issues and social action.

THE IMPACT OF
ORGANIZATIONAL FEATURES ON PRACTICE

One of the areas of curriculum content within what might be called behavioral science or social science is the nature of institutions and their impact on social work training and practice. These aspects of organizational theory have obvious relevance for deepened understanding of administration and social policy. Moreover, the habits of analysis of agency features call for, and reinforce, scientific-mindedness and ability to conceptualize.

What is meant by organizational features, and how may field teaching, in any setting, be related to this content?

The physical and social environments of any agency, particularly the ways in which client and social work roles are defined in relation to each other and to others in the agency, affect what students learn, what their attitudes to clients and others will be, and how they will behave or practice in relation to them. The consequences may be unintended in contrast with the planned consequences of the regular student training programs, but they may be equally significant. It is quite possible that what is unintentionally taught by the features of the setting conflicts with what is intentionally taught through field instruction. Operating side by side with a planned and explicit student training program, there is an unplanned and implicit educational process involved, with effects that may be neither anticipated nor desired. Identification and examination of key aspects of structure and organization, consciously included as part of field instruction, may reduce or redirect these effects and give focus to efforts to modify the structure where change effects are feasible and desirable. Examples will be given mainly from one type of agency, the mental hospital setting, because it is difficult to give examples from all types of organizational settings. It is hoped that this discussion will stimulate examination of the variety of settings in which field instructors teach. The goals would be to take what is relevant, to discard what is not relevant, and to add what is particularly significant to other types of settings.

The discussion begins with a consideration of certain physical features of institutional structure and their impact on student training and patient care.

Location in geographic isolation from communities in which patients live is one feature that tends to increase social-psychological distance between the patient and his community. Family and social contact is not readily managed as part of a treatment plan. In the geographically isolated setting, as contrasted with the neighborhood setting, the continuum of mental health and mental illness and the continuity between the hospital and the community are sometimes lost to sight. Hospitalization, as part of a cycle of community living, stress, hospital living, and return to the community, is more difficult to see. The familial and social context of mental illness becomes shadowy. The centralized social agency in the large urban community may share some of the same problems, though to a lesser degree.

Undoubtedly, many social service departments and field instructors have tried to deal with the narrow perspectives influenced by isolation, both through field teaching and administrative devices. It would be very useful if these were made an explicit part of field teaching.

Large size predisposes to a mass, custodial management approach rather than an individualized, differentiated approach. There is a sharp conflict between standardization and individualization. Many field instructors, consciously aware of the structural sources of these difficulties, have developed ways of teaching the relationship between organizational size and individualization. These instructors have contributed to policies and structures which have minimized the negative consequences of large size. Conceptualization and sharing of such experiences would be valuable.

Condition of physical facilities has an impact. Dilapidated physical facilities—an overcrowded, uncomfortable, dirty admission or intake office—may create a tendency for patients to think of themselves as dilapidated, unimportant, and hopeless. It is easier, even for social workers, to see the potentialities of patients when the physical setting is attractive and clean. Would it be useful in student training to generalize about the relationship of physical setting to psychological settings, as well as to consider how physical setting might be changed?

The social features of an institution or agency are more important than physical features. One such feature is the decision-making structure. One pattern is a highly centralized one in which authority is concentrated at top administrative or medical levels, and power flows in one direction from top to bottom through a hierarchy, with the patient or client as low man on the totem pole. In this type of authority structure, the patient is defined as unable to participate in, let alone make, decisions. The social structure teaches staff, students, and patients that patients are unable to make decisions at any level. The patient is exposed to both the social structure and staff attitudes and ultimately tends to take on their attitudes. A number of questions may be asked: Is a patient expected to obey? Does he have choices about his clothing and personal property? How much power does he have over his own life? Is it the very maximum he can use within his illness? To what extent has the institution defined the patient's responsibility for decisions in the light of therapeutic objectives?

Some of the same questions might, of course, be asked about the role of social work staff in decision making. If one of the goals of field instruction is to prepare students for ultimate professional autonomy, then it seems important to expose them to a model in which social work staff has a voice in the policies and practices of the agency.

It seems important to create conscious and explicit awareness of a decision-making structure, if only to modify the patient's perceptions which are derived from the relatively powerless roles in which they are often cast. It may be useful to teach students that every encounter that patients have with them has consequences for the patient's ability to make decisions, to be self-directing, and to develop self-esteem. The sheer importance of explaining things to patients and avoiding treatment of them as "specimens" on ward rounds may be underlined from this point of view.

In addition to the matter of understanding and adapting current ways of working, students may be exposed to efforts to change role relationships. Some examples from experiments in public welfare agencies may be of interest. The organization of a Client Advisory Committee to meet regularly with the administrator, the use of clients as volunteer caretakers for children accompanying parents at intake, and the formation of a client group to work up a manual listing the entitlements and procedures applicable to all clients have been successfully tried. Also, clients have been used in orienting new workers by sharing their ideas on helpful ways in which workers may relate to clients. These efforts constitute interesting alterations in role relationships and suggest new ways of working with clients in groups.

There are many other aspects of social structure that deserve attention: the patients' informal culture; the doctor, nurse, or attendant relationships with patients; and so on.

Organizational structure may be treated in a carefully planned sequence in the classroom. In the field, the rhythm of teaching and learning may be different. The field teacher alert to opportunities for illustrating or extending content in this area will find many ways to stimulate learning.

SCIENTIFIC INQUIRY IN THE FIELD CURRICULUM

The third area of content to be considered consists of social work research, or, to use a broader term, scientific inquiry in social work. The stated objectives of all schools of social work make it clear that educational goals of scientific inquiry are applicable for all students. It is generally assumed that these goals are not only appropriate for the research course, but for all academic courses and for field instruction. As with other areas of curriculum content, field instruction has a significant role to play. Field experiences represent for the student a look at what social work practice is really like. If field experiences are planfully related to what the student is learning in his research courses, he will be emotionally and intellectually able to incorporate a scientific orientation into his total professional outlook.

The author's view of what is involved in scientific inquiry is a broad one, and there may be some warranted differences with the conceptions to be outlined. Four closely related elements are involved: attitudes favoring scientific inquiry, some facility or skill in the processes of scientific inquiry, ability to think conceptually, and the linking of human welfare values to processes of scientific inquiry.

The latter two components have already been discussed. The ability to think conceptually is essential to scientific inquiry; and the field instructor who stimulates conceptual learning is making a substantial contribution to his student's research learning. A student who thinks in terms of clearly defined concepts and propositions can make an easy transition to understanding what is meant by research variables and to understanding hypotheses that make statements about relationships between variables formulated for the purpose of testing them. In connection with the prior discussion of social policy and agency structure, the link between policies, procedures, and structures on the one hand, and values on the other, has been stressed. The idea of analyzing the intended and unintended consequences of policies and structures has been mentioned; consequences only have meaning when related to values that guide judgments about the desirability of consequences.

In the attempt to describe what is meant by the scientific inquiry component, attention can be concentrated on attitudes and skills.

An attitude of scientific inquiry is based upon awareness of, and acceptance by, educators and students that much of social work knowledge is fragmentary or untested. This is not only true of social work but true of behavioral science and, perhaps to a lesser degree, true of natural science as well. Social workers have to live and practice and learn in the context of uncertainty and the hypothetical, rather than from a certain and fixed knowledge base. The corollary to this acceptance is an active curiosity about the unknown and unconfirmed, a desire to find out what is being discovered or tested, and a desire to participate within the limits of one's own knowledge and skill in these efforts. There is involved, too, a concern for evidence, and for valid inferences from evidence; a sense of accountability for one's own inferences as well as those of others. This attitude requires that both educators and students be willing to face change in their own ideas, and that they have a view of social work as a changing, not a static, profession. Scientific inquiry requires a problem-solving attitude characterized by independent and critical thinking.

Disciplines of scientific inquiry are related to these attitudes; indeed, these disciplines may be considered the behavioral manifestations of these attitudes. The profession expects to see scientific behavior manifested in direct work with people, in analysis of social policy and agency structure, in interested and critical appraisal of research efforts. It expects, in all these activities, demonstrated habits of exploration of evidence, thoughtfulness in drawing inferences, and conscious activity in testing inferences. Both within and beyond direct service activity, it hopes to see examination of phenomena from qualitative and quantitative points of view. So disciplines of scientific inquiry are not only applicable to special research efforts, but, in this conception at least, they should be applied to all professional practice and thinking.

How then, can field instruction contribute to research-mindedness and research skills? The question is first discussed in terms of what the field instructor can do with direct service assignments. In insisting on the necessity for getting information before arriving at an assessment of the problem, the field instructor can reinforce scientific habits of seeking evidence, and of relating inferences to evidences and logic. If the instructor emphasizes the tentative nature of diagnostic formulations, and points out that these are subject to verification in continuing relationships with clients or groups, and that they may change, he is teaching scientific principles. While the process of helping includes intuitive and emotional components, there is a core of scientific method. The helping process has many parallels with exploratory research. Both begin with a felt difficulty that is not fully defined; both involve gathering of possibly relevant information to assist in drawing of tentative inferences or hypotheses; and both involve attempts at later testing of these inferences.

The idea of "possibly relevant information" is of interest. Both in social work process and in a piece of research there is an underlying frame of reference; a set of ideas that guides the search for information. Both professional understanding and research are improved if these guiding assumptions about what is relevant are made explicit. Another consideration is that the set of ideas about relevant information is not fixed for all time. The field of inquiry in social work practice changes with new knowledge. If a student gets the sense of a field of inquiry, can guide his activity on this basis, and yet be aware that what is considered relevant changes with developing knowledge, he has mastered important scientific principles.

The examination of statistical data is an essential skill in the intelligent consumption of research material and in participation in research efforts. Does field instruction have anything to contribute? Students generally fill out statistical reports, which presumably form part of a total agency report and presumably accomplish a variety of purposes for agency administration. How much do students understand of the purposes of these reports and the variety of uses to which they are put? If the field instructor, alert to educational opportunities, explains the format and purposes of these reports, shows how they fit into the total agency report, and how they provide administrative guidance and facilitate agency interpretation, the student has been given valuable exercise in quantitative thinking as well as some insights into the administrative process. The educational point is that the student's positive motivation toward helping people can be usefully channeled as he is helped to see the connection between statistics and the efforts of the agency to increase its effectiveness in meeting needs. Hopefully, this kind of field instructor activity may dilute the phobic avoidance of statistics. Students, given assignments to describe the content and uses of agency statistical forms, develop surprising (to them) awareness of their interest and value, as well as awareness of their shortcomings and additional uses.

The agency as a whole can provide an atmosphere of interest in scientific inquiry by carrying on either modest and informal studies or formal research. The attitude of interest in discovery and testing is then more transmissible. Students may learn something about problems that need research and may generate research interests of their own. Students may, and should, be oriented to the particular agency studies that are going on, and to the designs and methodologies used. Perhaps the time is coming when a portion of the field learning time, for a student concentrating in casework, group work, or community organization, will be devoted to research assignments. Then research will no longer be considered something isolated from social work, or something done only by research experts from another planet. It is not assumed that all social workers should be able to direct research and carry on a research career; but it is assumed that all social workers are research-minded, able to review research intelligently, and have acquired simple research skills that enable them to participate in research under expert direction.

In summary, field instruction can assist in a desirable goal: a lessening of the distance between research and practice.

ORIENTATION TO CHANGE

There has already been a good deal of reference to "orientation to change" as an objective of field teaching. This is not surprising, for an orientation to change is, or should be, pervasive, and not separate from other content. In discussing the field teaching of content related to social policy, social services, and organizational structure, emphasis has been put on the importance of analysis, examination of consequences, identification of gaps and inadequacies, recognition of needs for change, and preparation for participation in change efforts. Similarly, with respect to scientific inquiry as a field component, there has been postulated a basic willingness to face change in one's own ideas and in the knowledge base of social work. To speak of the desirability of a positive orientation to change is to affirm seriously the nature of social work as a developing profession. Hence, separate discussion of this third criterion is not essential.

FIELD-CLASS FEEDBACK

The final criterion for professional field instruction is feedback of knowledge from field to class; a reverse addition to the usual principle that the field should reflect what goes on in the class curriculum. Field-class feedback, as a goal, is inseparable from conceptions of what the relation of class to field should be in professional education for social work. Historically, class teaching began as an academic extension of, and support to, experience in the field. There then developed a different conception, in which field and class experiences were seen as mutually interacting and supporting. This is the conception which underlies this paper. A third conception is now evidenced in beginning experimental efforts: field experiences should be viewed as laboratory extension and support of class experiences. It appears that field-class feedback is not likely to be emphasized in this new conception since the flow of content is so heavily from class to specially devised field experiences, a somewhat artificial concept considering what generally goes on in practice. A positive case can be made for this latter approach, but there are choices to be made.

The two-way reciprocal impact has not been sufficiently stressed in current conceptions of the nature of the relationships between class and field teaching and learning. Certainly, it is difficult to achieve feedback from field to class, more so than in the opposite direction. The reasons may be that mutual feedback cannot take place until conceptual teaching and learning, reflection of total curriculum, and orientation to change are truly characteristic of field instruction. But field practice and field instruction can produce generalized knowledge just as the school can. Research and scholarly writing can and does go on in either the agency or the school setting. Developments in the field may be ahead of those taught in classes in some ways, while in other ways conceptions and approaches taught in class may be ahead of those in the field.

If these statements are accepted, there remains the practical questions of what channels are available, or can be devised, to facilitate this feedback. Perhaps active efforts are needed by the school to identify newer developments in the field and to invite field instructors to present such developments to appropriate class-faculty groupings, such as curriculum committees. If there is a concern with encouragement of field-class feedback, a variety of effective devices will be found.

The criteria for professional field instruction are very difficult to achieve and, in a sense, are always striven for and never fully achieved. The coordinated efforts of all educators in class and field are needed to link research and theory, theory and practice, practice and curriculum.

LEARNING THEORIES AND PATTERNS IN BLOCK AND CONCURRENT FIELD INSTRUCTION

ALICE A. SELYAN

WE HAVE, as a profession, talked and written much about field instruction, emphasized its transcendent place in the education of the social work student, and struggled to find some model that would ensure its most effective implementation. At the very moment that we have totted up its firm positives, we have recognized the multiple variables in terms of setting, teaching personnel, opportunity, the intensity of the student-instructor relationship, and the meeting of diverse personalities which have made it an uncertain and, in considerable measure, an unpredictable learning experience for the student. Simultaneously, we have too often heard charges from the employing agencies that graduates were not adequately prepared for "responsible entry" into the profession.

Today, with the great proliferation of social work courses in undergraduate, community, and technological colleges and their incursion into field practice as part of their educational program, there is a pressing need to establish precisely the level and nature of field instruction experience at the master's level, distinguishing it from any other and meriting the additional two years of education. In this context, to do nothing more than recite theories or patterns related to block or concurrent plans of field instruction would seem to be no more than an idle exercise. This paper is presented, however, with the hope that it may make some slight contribution to ongoing considerations for future designs of field instruction experience.

ALICE A. SELYAN is a field instructor at Carleton University School of Social Work. This paper was originally presented at the Council on Social Work Education Sixteenth Annual Program Meeting in Minneapolis, Minnesota, January, 1968.

Any discussion of the block plan may begin with the frank admission that a primary reason for its adoption has been as much one of expediency as of its considered merits. In a survey conducted as part of a doctoral thesis in 1959, 11 respondents of the 13 block-plan schools indicated that lack of adequate or appropriate field placements in the vicinity of the school was a major factor leading to its choice, and that such choices were made either with the founding of the school—one as early as 1918—or at various intervals, as increased enrollment and expanding programs led to a plan alternate to the concurrent system in use.[1]

This might seem to argue that the block plan is a matter of pragmatic choice; but on further study it becomes clear that it has many intrinsic merits, some of them held in common with concurrent instruction, some unique to it. It is almost as though, having made a choice under the press of reality, one comes to realize and appreciate after the fact the gratuitous gifts that accompany the choice.

In seeking a dominant theme which might distinguish the block plan, one is struck with the relevance to it at varying levels of the concept of gestalt. In a sense, the student in the block plan is involved in a total way in a total environment and becomes, for a predetermined and specific period of time, a fully interacting part of that environment. The hazards of such an "immersion" are immediately evident as one contrasts it with the gradual, "part-time" introduction of the student in the concurrent plan, who moves in alternating identity from student in the classroom to student-professional in the agency. The responsibility of the field instructor for the block-plan student stands paramount in this situation. It is he, who, as an educator, must insure that the student does not take on the guise of "worker" (this becomes sometimes too easy if the student has had prior experience, or if there is a large complement of untrained workers in the agency) but clearly retains his role of learner, whose primary task is not the management of his cases, but a conceptual approach to the processes of treatment in which he will engage with his clients. Several internal and external conditions further serve to safeguard the student's experience. The assignment of a limited number of cases reduces the possibility of escape into activity for activity's sake, or of exclusive attention to operational skills, and brings to focus the need for a progressively deepening understanding of the nature of psycho-social dysfunctioning and the development of increasingly selective modes of intervention.

The consultative visits of school faculty to the instruction setting reaffirm the inherent relation of class and field, and make explicit as its

---

[1] Ruth Gilpin, "Some Aspects of the Structure and Development of Block Plan—Schools of Social Work," basis for a chapter in dissertation written for doctoral degree at University of Pennsylvania, entitled "Concurrence in the Block Plan for Social Work Education," 1959.

conjoint task the educational progress of the student. This purpose is repeated in the student's and field instructor's periodic evaluative reports, which constitute part of the overall educational diagnosis of the student, to the school. Further, course papers to be prepared during the field instruction term require the student to relate theory and practice in a concrete way.

Given this hazard of "immersion," and other hazards which will be touched upon at a later point, clear and firm advantages also emerge. The concept of gestalt might be applied to the block of class instruction which precedes entry into the field (and it will be noted that a number of concurrent schools also observe this plan). Within the school setting and before he is confronted with the task of *doing*, the student is involved in integrating—in the sense of making his own—a body of knowledge, which gives him first a broad overview of the field of practice in which he is to engage, and second, a more detailed exploration of that specific part which will be most relevant to his own immediate efforts in the field. An inherent and highly valuable aspect of learning is the evoking of and reflection on attitudes that derive, for the student, both from this body of knowledge and from identification with the bearer of that knowledge. During this period, there is an opportunity to integrate in a reflective way[2] the several parts of that knowledge made available to him through his own involvement in class and book, and there is also an opportunity to establish some beginning sense of his own professional identity. (Attitudes, which are challenging and challenged, are made more clearly his own.) In the light of this, it may be said that the student in the block plan is afforded some greater sense of wholeness as he enters field instruction. It may also be argued that this will not have any reality until it is tested out in the actual arena of practice.

The need for some ordered progression in the field learning experience has long been emphasized, although its actual realization is too frequently in question. It is predicated that this aspect of the block plan (i.e., this sense of an integrated wholeness) expedites or facilitates this progression. The student, having been given some prior overview of the professional role, moves with his instructor's guidance more consciously and purposefully into that specific part which is his immediate task, traversing territory which conceptually and attitudinally, at least in some measure, is familiar to him, and which bears relevance

---

[2] In the particular school that the writer represents, small integration seminars are held during the first academic term with the purpose of encouraging students in this group to question and clarify their understanding of class content, to seek out the interrelated elements of the curriculum, to respond attitudinally to material that has been presented, to make some beginning in self-awareness, and, not least, to experience the process of supportive and challenging group interaction as a part of their learning.

in time and place to the total design of the helping process. (At the same time that this claim is made on behalf of the block plan, it must be added that the student's "foreknowledge" touches on only a small part of the problem of an ordered progression of learning in the field— a problem that remains complex and the feasibility of which is often in question in relation to the immediate reality of the clients' needs and the agency's responsibilities to him. It will be recalled, parenthetically, that these matters were discussed at CSWE's National Curriculum Workshop Conference in 1960 and some opinions were proffered by Tyler[3] at that time and by Towle[4] in 1952. The problem has continued to hold the attention of school and field. Basic to and inseparable from this difficulty is that encountered in the attempts of schools to establish a definitive curriculum content of field instruction. Schubert,[5] among others, has given valuable help in identifying the critical components of the content of field instruction.)

It might be assumed that the weight of such prior knowledge could generate a paralyzing kind of anxiety in the student. However, experience has shown that it affords a certain sense of realistic security and serves as a challenge, which is reflected most often in the student as an eagerness to test out knowledge, skills, and, most vitally, the self. Tyler speaks of the learner being required "to stretch" to attain levels of achievement which are beyond his immediate reach, yet within his ultimate capacity.[6]

Having introduced the student to the agency, one may briefly pursue his course through his period of placement—a period which varies from school to school, from blocks of six weeks to eight-and-a-half months, with all manner of combinations of plans, in the first and second year.[7] The student's overall pattern is marked by the universally

---

[3] *Building the Social Work Curriculum*, Report of the National Curriculum Workshop, Allerton, Illinois, 1960 (New York: Council on Social Work Education, 1960). For Tyler's discussion *re* the matter of progression in learning, see pp. 35-50.

[4] Charlotte Towle, "The Distinctive Attributes of Education for Social Work," in *A Source Book of Readings on Teaching in Social Work: Reprints of Selected Articles* (New York: Council on Social Work Education, 1965), pp. 13-14.

[5] Margaret Schubert, "Curriculum Policy Dilemmas in Field Instruction," *Journal of Education for Social Work*, Vol. 1, No. 2 (Fall, 1965), pp. 27-34.

[6] *Building the Social Work Curriculum, op. cit.,* p. 37.

[7] Annette Garrett, "Learning Through Supervision," Smith College Studies in Social Work, Vol. 24 (February, 1954), pp. 3-109.
It is important to note Garrett's broad definition of a block plan of learning. She questioned whether block field instruction could achieve its potentials without a similar complement of block academic work, and expressed doubt that the addition of a block of field instruction to a primarily concurrent plan could yield an integrated educational program. In similar vein, one might ask whether a brief six-week block of field instruction does more than accept

observed cyclic or rhythmic design that characterizes all growth or change. The initial period of eagerness coupled with anxiety in the average student finds concrete expression in the effort to integrate with the task of *doing* knowledge and attitudes derived from prior and current learning, and, more essentially, in a trial-and-error use of self. Not uncommonly, the student's first entry is characterized as one in which he, rather than the client, is the protagonist. Unconsciously, his needs, anxieties, and urgency to prove himself in order to test out the magic of his caring and newly acquired learning stand pre-eminent. Only gradually, as he experiences some evidences of his competence (however modest), finds acceptance and approval of instructor and client alike, entertains the possibility of error, and learns something of the pain and growth that come with understanding of self, is he truly free to perceive and respond to the client in his reality. It is then that he can more fully move from self to other and use himself more consciously, more purposefully, on behalf of his client. This interval appears to be followed, in turn, by a plateau, or even by a seeming regression or retreat—a period of questioning and questing, when energies are replenished and re-deployed for further movement toward a new level of accomplishment. In relation to the length of the field instruction, a second such period may appear some weeks before termination; it is generally briefer and followed by a more marked and integrated thrust in the grasp of use of skills and self. The determinants of this final push are interesting to conjecture—is it the need to prove oneself once and for all, the need to give all that one has to clients who have come to have deep and real meaning, and the need to assuage part of the guilt that arises at abandoning the clients as they have so often been abandoned before? The leaving of the agency and the return to an academic period of time in the school—and this seems to be the common pattern —stir up mingled feelings of regret over separation from the agency and its associations. A conflict of feelings arises around the resumption of the role of the student in the classroom, now seen as somewhat inferior to that held in the agency of student-professional. But, equally, there is keen realization that he, the student, has done as much as he can for the moment with the armamentarium that is his, and he is eager now to advance to a new level of knowing, of awareness, of becoming.

Entry into the second-year field placement is at a more sophisticated level, although it may be marked by a curious, though happily brief, lag in relation to the finishing point of the previous year. This seems

a form in name only. Can it offer more than minimal opportunity for those specific experiences that a longer unbroken and continuing period of time affords? Having said this, one is immediately assailed with the problem of the optimum related lengths of time of class to field, an area that the writer will, on this occasion, gladly leave unanswered.

to be brought about by the anxiety of a new setting, by the perceived expectations for achievement at a more advanced level, and by a certain resistance at having to resume once again the more dependent role of student-professional under the surveillance of the instructor and school. This is more real if the student, in the vacation interval, has worked in an agency where he enjoyed considerably more independence and freedom as an employee. The balance of the field practice term may repeat, but in attenuated form, the cycle of the previous year. In the normally adequate student, however, there are progressively increasing insights, greater flexibility and creativity in the use of his skills, and a more differential use of self—in all, an integration of the various growth processes into the professional person who stands on the threshold of "responsible entry."

This overall pattern may, in most respects, be little different than that of any other plan of placement. There would appear to be empirical evidence, however, that the continuous, relatively uninterrupted, undivided, and, hence, more total involvement in terms of time, requirements, and relationships within the block term in the agency, contribute to an earlier and more firm consolidation of knowledge and skills and a clearer and surer emergence of the role of the professional self.

Several themes emerging from this statement may be pursued. For one, the full-time presence of the student in the agency exposes him to a wide range of learning opportunities, both in the agency itself and in the related community, in which, in a selective and purposeful way, he may participate. There is learning and growing through the process of osmosis—in being a continuing observer of and/or a participant in the day-to-day operation of the agency, its moods and tenor, the realities of its problems, and the pattern of its transactional relationships as a community. Is there not, implicit in all this, a more sustained opportunity to have reflected in a significant and substantial way, the total curriculum of the school in the practice setting—a learning experience to be made more explicit by the Field Instructor? These are peripheral, though no less important themes of the learning-growing process arising in conditions, in degree, more specific to the block instruction plan.

Of much greater and fundamental significance to all learning-growing is the fact of relationship, whether it is perceived in terms of the child in the nurturing growth-promoting relationships within his family, or, in this particular instance, of the social work student in the context of professional education. Historically, the roots of this concept lie in all considerations of human relationships; Towle[8] and Taft,[9] among many others of note, have spoken and written of it. Towle, in an early article, wrote "There is growing recognition among educators that within

---

[8] Towle, *op. cit.*, pp. 9-12.
[9] Jessie Taft, "The Concepts of the Growth Process Underlying Social Work Practice," *Social Casework*, Vol. 31, No. 8 (October, 1950), pp. 311-318.

a professional school the individual and collective teaching, helping, administering relationship with the student is the core of his preparation for professional relationship. This relationship, in the context of which knowledge and skills [and, one would like to add, attitudes][10] are conveyed, determines in large measure the learner's capacity to work purposefully with people in ways appropriate to the profession, whether in the helping relationship between practitioner and recipient. . . ."[11]

Bowers, in a recent statement, speaks of the central theme of relationship as the foundation of social work practice and understanding and awareness of relationship as pivotal to social work education.[12]

Has this relationship of which we speak—between student and field instructor and other associates, and between student and client—any significant difference in the two field instruction plans? In both situations, may we accept that the student will be helped to grow both personally and professionally in the accepting-challenging relationship with the instructor? He will grow through identification within that relationship with the instructor, and through increasing self-awareness stimulated and supported again within the relationship; he will achieve a clearer and more specific definition of his own individuality as an emerging professional person. Such a relationship—and it may well be enriched by association with other professional persons in the agency or community—will hopefully coincide with and confirm those derived in relationships with the classroom teacher or school advisor.[13] The writers who have been cited (and mention should also be made of Paul Halmos[14] and Bernard Bandler[15]) emphasize that it is in the vital experiencing of this enabling, growth-producing relationship that the student

---

[10] Writer's added note.

[11] Towle, op. cit.

[12] Swithun Bowers, "Objectives of Carleton University School of Social Work and Their Planning Implications." Statement prepared for intra-university use (Ottawa, 1967).

[13] The relationship of the student with his faculty advisor in the first academic term of the block plan may provide him with a valuable personal experience in the helping-growing process and prepare him not only for a like relationship with the field instructor but also provide some part of a model for his relationship with his clients. Peripherally, the relationship may yield early significant insights of the student's potential for educational and personal growth. The opportunity for such a relationship will depend in good part on the ratio of faculty to student, and, in greater measure perhaps, on the school's conviction about the place and worth of this experience for the student.

[14] Paul Halmos, *The Faith of the Counsellors* (London: Constable and Co., 1965).

[15] Bernard Bandler, "Ego-Centered Teaching," *Ego-Oriented Casework: Problems and Perspectives*, Howard J. Parad and Roger R. Miller, eds. (New York: Family Association of America, 1963).

can understand and seek to bring such help to his clients. Jessie Taft has written, "To believe in the possibility of growth for the client, one has to have known the release of growth in the self, through help consciously sought and professionally controlled."[16]

Against this rather optimum picture of the student-instructor relationship, there arise, not unnaturally, difficulties within that relationship—those sparked by elements of transference and, it must be added, counter-transference. Latent, residual, or unresolved struggles around dependence, independence, authority, and self-identity, emerge and find expression.

Similarly, the relationship with the client may reactivate, in serious measure, old problems or create new ones which exceed the student's competence and tolerance and deeply shake his trust in himself. In both instances, the demands now on the student-instructor relationship require of the instructor greater skill, more sensitive and accurate educational diagnosis of the nature of the difficulties, and knowledge of the appropriate measures to be taken. The many varying responses of the student in such circumstances are familiar to us—inappropriate dependence or aggressive independence, depression, resistance to the suggestion of self-awareness, hostility actively or passively expressed, projections, rationalizations, etc.

In these circumstances, that are trying for field instructor of concurrent and block plan alike, are there any significant differences? It is suggested that the field instructor in the block-placement plan may be in a better position to formulate an earlier and more firm educational diagnosis for his student. He will be aided in this by the observations, already communicated to him, of school faculty during the prior classroom period, and by the fact that the student's constant and continuing presence in the agency projects a composite image of the patterns of relationship and of interaction with varying peoples and in diverse situations.

More significantly, it is proposed that, for the student in the block-placement plan, the sustained relationship with one central model (the field instructor), uninterrupted by regular departures to the school with association with its personnel, makes for a more intense and meaningful experience. Moreover, the student's primary task for this given period is not divided between achievement in class and field. The task is concentrated on success or failure in the field, and the instructor becomes a key figure. If this position be accepted, both disadvantages and advantages may be readily perceived. If there are strong negative transference and counter-transference factors present, or, more simply, a clash of personalities, the very intensity of the relationship may render it unproductive for student and instructor alike. On the other hand,

---

[16] Taft, *op. cit.*, p. 312.

there is some possibility that this very intensity may constitute a strong drive to seek understanding and resolution of its negative components. The possibility of a fostered and prolonged dependency in the more intense relationship may be suggested and can be real, if the instructor does not, like a good parent, encourage and help develop increasing professional self-reliance.

If, on the other hand, the student-instructor relationship is basically a positive one, its intensity may prove a most effective agent in stimulating and sustaining the student through the often painful process of growth and through the critical experiences of self-awareness and change. Furthermore, identification with the professional person of the instructor will be strong and at a mature level, and have little or none of the negative identification with the feared or disliked figure of authority.

To return once more to the theme of gestalt, the student's continuing role as worker for his clients, uninterrupted by his simultaneous return to his role as student in the classroom, may contribute to a more active feeling of responsibility for his clients and to a deeper and more constant investment of himself in his relationships with them. Hopefully, then, these relationships will reflect some part of that sustaining and challenging stimulus to growth which he himself has experienced in his relationship with his field instructor.

What potential uses does the block plan of instruction offer? One might note the possibility of numerically increased placements, but for graduate schools to think only in terms of numbers, however pressing the need, is virtually to stand still. Does the relatively constant set of block field instruction lend itself to research studies and experimentation, whether concerning the student's learning experience, his practice, or his relationship? And, if such study is possible or fruitful, can such findings, in addition to that which we already know of the block plan, make some meaningful contribution for the future?

We have noted our need to distinguish with far greater specificity the basic ways in which the level of graduate field instruction is to differ from that of undergraduate and other plans of learning in the field. We have long been aware that the multiple variables of our present plans of field instruction—whether block or concurrent—reflect too many of the more undesirable vestiges of the apprenticeship system and cannot insure that challenging, productive planned experience in which concept and skill, theory and doing find their fullest integration.

If we are to break ourselves free and search for new models,[17] one answer might be found in a system of "internship" which would use

---

[17] Mildred Sikkema, "A Proposal for an Innovation in Field Learning and Teaching," *Field Instruction in Graduate Social Work Education: Old Problems and New Proposals* (New York: Council on Social Work Education, 1966).

the "continuous" gestalt theme of the block plan, which would be internal to the master's program—most suited, perhaps, to the objectives of first-year instruction—situated in the university setting, and having a planfully structured program of learning and doing.

What, in summary, have we said about the learning experience in the block plan of instruction? If we once again consider the applicability of the concept of gestalt to learning—a learning that, in our context especially, is not just an exercise of the mind but involves the whole staff, changing, growing, becoming—we must perceive the environment in which this process takes place as an integral part of that learning. It may be held, then, that the essentially intact, uninterrupted, and undivided environment of the block plan of instruction both helps to create and to constitute a vital part of a continuing, consistent, and intense experience in learning. Two major considerations seem to arise: first, that the block plan, providing, as it were, a psychologically undivided and a more emotionally intact experience, leaves the student free to apply and involve himself more deeply in the learning-doing-becoming task. It is suggested, on empirical evidence only, that this appears to result in accelerated and more consolidated competence in practice. But by the very same token, this "total" experience in the field setting raises the risk of diluting the conceptual component which marks it as an educational requirement at the university level. To guard against such a possibility, school and field must collaborate closely in identifying clearly delineated objectives of the student's education, and, much more difficult, in seeking together the learning means and experiences that will ensure these goals.

If we further apply the concept of this "totality" to the student-client system, we may see that the experiential climate created for the student in this continuous setting is extended to the client (and here we are echoing Taft) so that, in the transactional relationship, there may be possibility for a deeper, more complete sense of involvement on both sides. Such investment may be rewarded with gratification as there is a perceived change in the client's condition.

Where this does not occur in commensurate measure, particularly for the beginning or less mature student, frustration, self-doubt, anger, or despair may follow. It is a hard lesson that every student must ultimately learn—that all the knowledge he has, bonded with love and caring, may not be enough. Yet, we as instructors and teachers, whether of concurrent or block plan, would agree—to misquote a familiar phrase—it is better that they have this love, even if they lose. Swithun Bowers, in a talk to the graduating class in 1961 on the fundamental nature of the helping relationship, saw as its essence "two-interwoven elements, knowing and loving, a loving that springs forth from a knowing," and he went on to say that this implied "some kind of union, some kind of unity between the knower and the known, between the lover and the loved."[18] This he saw as the nature of the activity for which the student was prepared, and to which he ultimately went forth as a professionally helping person.

To end on such a note, to speak of love in this very scientific age and in this highly academic setting may seem naively simple, or even trite. But, indeed, is not this loving the very core, the very ancient roots of our profession of social work? And although the words we use make love sound a simple thing, is it not so complex in its realization that we have yet truly to achieve it. For essential to the notion of loving is the essential element of the giving of one's self. For the student this is a lesson hard to learn; for the instructor, no less hard to teach.

---

[18] Swithun Bowers, Address to Graduating Class, *News Letter*. The Alumni Association of the University of Ottawa School of Social Welfare, June, 1961.

THE POTENTIAL OF CONCURRENT FIELD INSTRUCTION FOR LEARNING

MARGARET L. SCHUTZ

ALTHOUGH I come from a school of social work which, since its inception in 1925, has held consistently to a plan of concurrent field instruction, I will not be arguing the merits of concurrent field instruction as superior to block field instruction. I suspect that both plans, in many instances, began not as a result of evidence gained from empirical study, or even as the result of a strong educational theoretical position, and I suspect that both will probably continue, as the result of historical or geographical accident, regardless of the specific merits of either. Nevertheless, it would seem profitable to explore how we might better capitalize on the particular characteristics of each of these plans as a means toward more effective social work education. Some of what I wish to say might also be equally applicable to block field instruction. It is my contention that concurrent field instruction does offer some unique opportunities for learning, but we have not exploited them as fully as we might.

To assess either, or any kind of field instruction, we need to start with a fairly realistic appraisal of where we are in social work education today with respect to field instruction. There is no question that we discovered and developed a good thing in field instruction, as demonstrated by the fact that our students in the past have learned to practice respectably, and the employing agencies have sought them as good beginning practitioners. Other disciplines, notably medicine and law, have come to copy some of our patterns of field experience, but, until

MARGARET L. SCHUTZ is an associate professor and director of Field Instruction at the George Warren Brown School of Social Work of Washington University. This paper was originally presented at the Council on Social Work Education Sixteenth Annual Program Meeting in Minneapolis, Minnesota, January, 1968.

about five years ago, we had not seriously questioned or substantially changed our basic pattern of field instruction despite many changes in practice and in education. The half-million-dollar Council on Social Work Education Curriculum Study did not include field instruction in its purview. We must also face the fact that in the past few years we have been bombarded with a knowledge explosion in the behavioral sciences—some fallout from which is thought to be applicable to social work practice—and we have been faced with great pressure to expand our fields of practice and extend our method of intervention. We are also under pressure to increase the efficiency and reduce the cost of field education as evidenced by efforts to reduce the hours per week, increase the number of students per field instructor, and even shorten the two-year requirement for the master's degree.

In order to handle these current and pressing developments and respond without a reduction of standards, or, more positively, to capitalize on what we think are the strengths of social work field instruction, we are required to be much more sophisticated as educators than I believe we generally are. At the least, we need to be clearer about our educational assumptions and the rationales we have for changing some things and for not changing others.

A review of recent literature, which it was hoped might be a useful guide in this matter, revealed how limited our actual knowledge is of how people learn, particularly adults. The literature was not very helpful in providing an educational basis for teaching in the field. Some suggestions relating to teaching and learning in the field seemed almost an extension of the casework method—almost a therapeutic approach, with considerable stock placed on the importance of the relationship between field instructor and student as the most important ingredient in field learning—with great emphasis on affective learning. These are important elements in field teaching and learning, but scarcely form adequate underpinnings for all that must be considered professional learning in the field.

While I am certainly no expert in learning theory, examination of the literature left me convinced that theory in this area is inadequate as a guide for understanding and structuring learning in social work field instruction. Certainly, there is evidence to suggest that programmed learning plans have been most useful for acquiring certain information, and that encouraging results have been obtained in situations in which one behavior was substituted for another (perhaps we should look into this for some aspects of social work education). However, available learning theory provides insufficient guides for the complex type of learning required for professional social work practice and cognition or cognitive learning receives insufficient emphasis. It cannot, therefore, provide a basis for the knowledge-guided practice claimed as a requirement for truly professional social work practice.

Have we stopped to consider what we mean by knowledge-guided practice and how we go about achieving it? What do we know about how people make the connection between the knowledge they are expected to command and the expected professional behavior that results from application of that knowledge? How do we know when professional behavior is truly guided by knowledge, and how do we get from the stage of knowing to the stage of acting in accordance with what we know? Have we not, all too often in social work, offered material to students in the classroom which we charge them to get hold of, and then offered them assignments in the field, usually in the form of cases or groups for professional service, and hoped that somehow what they learned in the classroom might have at least some applicability to what they were expected to do in the field situations? Or, have we not sometimes required the student to carry out certain activities in the field and then asked him to tell us what knowledge guided him—perhaps thus encouraging him to offer a rationalization for his behavior rather than a rationale? Even though we do not know for sure what it takes to get from the state of knowing to the state of practice that is truly knowledge-guided, is it possible to consider some stages that would give us clues to planning suitable learning experiences that might make this connection? For several years some of us at the George Warren Brown School of Social Work have been working on the assumption that there is a progression of learning that moves from the stage of mastery of knowledge through a stage of gaining true understanding of that knowledge, and only after that to the stage where one can actually engage in activity that is guided by that knowledge. We have spoken of this progression as "knowing," "understanding," and "doing."[1]

The question has been raised about the place of "affective" learning in this progression, and I would suggest that both affective and cognitive aspects are present in all three stages, if full learning is to take place. However, the first stage, "knowing," is more heavily weighted on the cognitive side, whereas "understanding" is somewhat more heavily weighted on the affective side, and "doing" is a blend of the two that results in effective knowledge-guided practice. It is my strong opinion, supported by review of the literature, that the cognitive aspects of learning, which we are suggesting as essential for knowledge-guided practice, have been much neglected in field learning, and that we have not taken full advantage of the unique opportunities in the field for providing experiences suitable to furthering progression in learning. In an educational scheme which provides for both class and field instruction, we would expect that the major part of the "knowing" stage would take place in the classroom, and that major development of understanding

---

[1] Margaret L. Schutz, "Report of the Field Instruction Experimental Project at the George Warren Brown School of Social Work," paper presented at the Fourteenth Annual Program Meeting of the Council on Social Work Education, New York, 1966.

and the learning of necessary behaviors for applying that understanding are uniquely the province of field instruction. I should point out that by "knowing" I am referring to the firm grasp of those generalizations in social work which might be considered technically as knowledge (in the sense of proven facts) and putative knowledge (in the sense of hypotheses to be studied), and also to those generalizations stemming from our value assumptions, which we hold to firmly as guideful to practice. It seems as important, in a profession as heavily value-based as social work, that students "know" fully those value assumptions that are expected to guide their practice, as it is that they "know" facts about human development, or theoretical assumptions concerning human behavior. Also, encompassed within "knowing" is command of the major practice principles necessary for successful intervention. I am referring to such things as obtaining a real hold of the hackneyed, but fundamental principle, "start where the client is." When truly "learned," this principle contains many important elements, such as obtaining enough knowledge about a client *and* his situation to provide a pretty good picture of "where he is," or finding ways of becoming involved in the client-process that are easy and non-disruptive but still firm enough to be helpful and effective. In other words, some of our simply stated practice principles have much in them that must be "known" before they can be skillfully applied.

If we can accept this view of learning in stages, and that to be fully "learned" each requires different and planned learning experiences, we will have a particularized notion of field instruction and its goals, as well as a special view of the opportunity it affords for achieving its objectives. This view suggests that field instruction be considered a special method of teaching-learning, in which opportunity is provided for bringing knowledge to bear upon reality situations. It suggests a somewhat different approach to planning for field learning situations from that of considering field instruction as a simulated practice experience in an agency in which, hopefully, some of the student's classroom learning might be applicable. Learning assignments in field instruction are probably structured in a particular way if one views field instruction as a place for "seating in" the knowledge gained from classroom and reading, as a place for the student to learn to become conscious of the conditions under which particular knowledge is most applicable, and as a place for him to learn to recognize the theoretical base of practice in a given situation so that he can apply it more effectively later on.

If the aim is to help students become professional social workers rather than agency employees familiar with one field of practice or a specific agency operation or skillful in one or more methods of intervention, then the plan for field instruction will reflect this aim. Needless to say, the ideas that the student is expected to utilize in his practice will guide the planning of learning experiences in the field. This view of learning obviously suggests both the advantages of and the necessity for an especially close "integration" between class and field. Perhaps our ever-present concern about "integration" between class and field results from the hiatus we have created by giving insufficient thought to the manner in which a student moves from acquisition of knowledge to knowledge-guided practice. We may have offered him two curricula— one for classroom and one for field—with a hoped-for, but not guaranteed, connection between the two.

The same framework for social work practice necessarily underlies all curriculum planning, whether in class or field, and the "integraters" to be employed are the major ideas. It is obvious that these concepts must be clearly identified, since they must provide the structure formerly supplied by the case or group assignment. It also seems clear that they must be related, since research has shown that unrelated things are learned more slowly and retained less well than related things. They must be reasonably limited in number if they are to be reinforced sufficiently in the field to achieve our goal. Concurrent field instruction seems to offer especially suitable arrangements for encouraging this view of learning.[2]

Perhaps now it would be helpful to turn to an illustration from our own experience which will suggest how concurrent field instruction might be most effectively utilized in support of this view of learning. In its Field Instruction Research Project, our school has been developing a practice framework derived from the original NASW Working Definition of Social Work Practice.[3] We have tried to set forth some major concepts which social workers might find useful in approaching any potential practice situation. Its present form and wording may not ultimately be the best for general use, but the central ideas seem to have merit as underpinning for all social work practice. Briefly, we start from the notion that the goal of all social work practice is the realization of the potential of every human being. To help achieve that goal, social work's major perspective is to focus on producing the kinds of transactions between the coping behaviors of people and the environmental situations with which they have to deal, and which will result in positive feedback for all involved. In other words, social work is concerned with what happens to people as individuals, in their day-to-day living, and with helping to achieve a "good match" between their coping behaviors

---

[2] The importance of stressing the underlying structure of what we want people to know, and teaching at a high level of generalization, which is applicable in many situations, is given strong support in Jerome S. Bruner's volume *The Process of Education* (Cambridge, Mass.: Harvard University Press, 1961).

[3] Harriett M. Bartlett, "Toward Clarification and Improvement of Social Work Practice," *Social Work*, Vol. 15, No. 2 (April, 1958), pp. 3-18; William E. Gordon, "A Critique of the Working Definition," *Social Work*, Vol. 19, No. 4 (October, 1962), pp. 3-13.

and their environments so that the transactions between will result in mutual benefit for both the individual and his environment.

Obviously, such a perspective leaves open such matters as the choice among theoretical explanations of human behavior, or the choice of particular techniques for effecting transactions: whether to work with individuals or with groups in relation to their coping behavior, or with community groups to effect environmental changes, or with policy-making groups in order to lead to more desirable outcomes for larger numbers, etc. But it does specify a framework and some basic notions, and it provides the broad limits in which to develop further knowledge. It maintains a central social work focus, on both individuals and environment, and may keep us from being buffeted about by fads, as often happens in social work.

Let me now illustrate the opportunities to promote the learning of these basic ideas in concurrent field instruction. Having been presented in class and in assigned reading with this conceptual framework, the Project students have then been set to view a wide variety of field situations from this perspective. For example, in observing a number of babies in a nursery for the newborn, students immediately noticed the difference in their coping behaviors at that young age, and could recognize different environmental stresses as they saw the babies with their mothers. They saw, perhaps, an extremely warm, loving, young mother with no income, no clothing for the baby, and an extremely inadequate living arrangement, or a frightened, teen-age, unmarried parent, completely resentful of the baby, yet somehow not choosing to give him up. Students can begin thinking about the kinds of transactions that might improve outcomes, or they may be asked to concentrate only on the idea of "coping behavior" itself, by noting variations in coping behavior between babies, school-age children, mentally retarded adolescents, severely disabled adults, etc. When students are assigned field observational experiences, they learn to relate concepts to specific situations, and to view situations from a social work perspective, thereby strengthening their identification with the profession, and firming up essential knowledge ingredients for later use in practice.

Students have found such a plan of reinforcement helpful to them as they moved into service-giving responsibilities. Field instructors using this framework also found greater degree of student confidence in service-giving situations. The timing of learning opportunities in the field theoretically can be planned very effectively with classroom presentations, provided the field faculty and the classroom faculty together work on curriculum planning. To the extent that we have been able to plan together the curriculum in our field instruction research project, we would suggest that such concurrence is workable. Some schools, notably the University of Southern California and San Diego State College, have been able to go much farther than we have in planning a total class and field curriculum around an agreed-upon perspective of social work practice. Unless a common base and a common curriculum are adopted, with class and field faculty working it out together, the potentially desirable features of concurrent field instruction—simultaneous class and field assignments, immediate feedback, immediate correctives and flexibility in timing—cannot be fully utilized.

Some learning principles rather readily applicable in concurrent field instruction are: reinforcement, particularly reinforcement in a relatively short period of time following original learning; partializing of the learning task into pieces small enough for effective grasp; opportunity to apply the "parts" in the framework of the whole; opportunity for application of knowledge in a variety of situations; and opportunities for immediate evaluation of the extent of learning and for applying correctives where needed. Possibly the greatest advantage is being able to plan learning experiences in the field far closer in time to cognitive learning of the elements of knowledge. Immediate opportunities to put some aspects of knowledge to use suggest a potentially fuller grasp of them and the eventual development of a readiness for application to a wide range of situations in service to people.

If partializing is a sound learning principle, then gaining a firm grasp of knowledge in pieces as one moves along, provided the pieces are seen in a context of the whole, should enable the student to have many pieces available for use in a live situation requiring full service responsibility. The opportunity for immediate feedback can point to knowledge that has not been fully grasped and can provide opportunities for both classroom and field instructors to introduce new experiences to strengthen the learning of a given concept. Teaching and/or learning knowledge-guided practice requires student awareness of the knowledge, values, and methods he calls upon to achieve results and is necessary in order to facilitate duplication in the variety of unfamiliar situations he will face within his professional career.

One result of our view of field learning is a suggested delay in full service responsibilities in field instruction. This may seem to be an argument for the block plan, which generally affords considerable delay in this area. However, what I am speaking about does not suggest a delay in applying all knowledge but rather relates to providing reinforcement in the field through opportunity for application of partialized aspects of learning. Delay in the carrying of full service responsibility has been incorrectly described as "delayed field instruction," or "orientation to field instruction," on the assumption that only case-carrying or group-serving offers true learning opportunities in the field. Our experimental field instruction project strongly suggests otherwise and supports the idea that a great many important aspects of "knowing," "understanding," and "doing," can be learned by students through assignments other than case-carrying or group-serving. Learning to approach persons of a socio-economic level different from one's own, learning the meaning of the impact of a particular community upon its residents, learning about the vast differences in coping behaviors of people in any given "category," such as newborn babies, mentally ill persons, or mentally retarded children, all of which take place in live situations, to which students bring some concepts about growth and development, about community organization, about social structures, coping behaviors, etc., add immeasurably to knowing, to understanding, and to a beginning level of doing. Such learning provides the student with excellent tools for moving into service-giving responsibility at a later date. If a student can be exposed in the classroom to considerable material on one of the value positions in social work, such as respect for the human dignity of every individual, and can then have several assignments in the field in which he is required to demonstrate this value by giving attention, support, and perhaps even physical comfort to a person who, for example, may be drunk, dirty, unshaven, essentially unable to communicate, then the student begins to realize the true meaning of this value position and begins to make it his own. If he can do this before he is required to provide full social work services to such a person, he is free to really dig in and understand the meaning of the idea. If he is required too early to give full "profesional social work service," he may be pushed beyond his comprehension of primary social work values. Concurrent field instruction does not automatically provide such opportunities, but it is well able to do so in a situation in which reinforcement and feedback enable student and class and field instructors to isolate those pieces of knowledge and those particular values over which the student must gain greater mastery.

It seems to me there can be a real danger in a long delay between presentation of knowledge content and opportunity to confront reality with it. If the student does not have to put to use anything of his knowledge or value system until he has a great bulk of it accumulated, it could conceivably be more difficult for him to sort out and go to work on the pieces of the "whole" with which he has trouble, and where he is hung up in the progression of learning, from knowing to understanding to doing. When the focus of field effort is on the service rendered, or on the outcomes of the service, and the student has no particular reinforcement of the knowledge that he is expected to apply, it is very easy to overlook identification and analysis of the behaviors, knowledge, and values that did, in fact, contribute to the outcomes achieved. There may be ways of overcoming this in the block plan, but there is built-in opportunity in concurrent field instruction, which, in our own school, we are striving to utilize more fully.

The importance of focusing on the major outlines of the social work perspective rather than on innumerable details needs stressing. A lockstep arrangement between class and field, even if practicable, would seem unduly rigid and restrictive. If, however, some broad underpinnings and major superstructure are laid down early at a sufficiently high level of generalization, then both the student and field instructor are in the happy position of being free for considerable individualization. There is ample room for the creativity of the field instructor, for the individual pace of student learning, for introduction of material and situations too difficult for the average student, but suitable for the most capable. Within the boundaries established, both student and field instructor are free to bring in knowledge, theoretical considerations, and practice principles and to test them out in increasingly complicated and varied ways.

Without such guidelines the student and field instructor are in the uncomfortable and unhappy position of being pulled and hauled toward any piece of knowledge or theory to which the student becomes attracted, and/or which his field instructor permits him to try out. There is a temptation for both student and field instructor to view the field instructor himself as the "guide" to be emulated. There is danger that both will find the boundaries of the student's learning determined more by the functions and policies of the agency in which he is placed or by the capacities and knowledge of the field instructor than by the boundaries of the major perspectives of social work practice.[4]

Concurrent field instruction offers a wealth of opportunity for helping a student gain a thorough grasp of basic knowledge essential to professional practice. It enables the school to recognize quickly both the learning problems of individual students and of the student body as a whole. Sometimes the form and timing of classroom presentations or the form and timing of field assignments made for the purpose of developing, understanding, and applying that knowledge are not as effective as they might be. Knowing this sooner rather than later offers the possibility of altering assignments in both class and field in a way appropriate to the objectives sought. This, hopefully, can move us more rapidly to the development of the knowledge-guided practitioners I believe our MSW graduates need to be, both now and in the future.

---

[4] Harriett M. Bartlett, "Characteristics of Social Work," *Building Social Work Knowledge,* Report of a Conference (New York: National Association of Social Workers, 1964).

A PRE-STRUCTURED AND FACULTY-DIRECTED APPROACH TO PRACTICE SKILL DEVELOPMENT

JACK ROTHMAN

INTRODUCTION

In this paper I will discuss various ideas concerning field instruction that have emerged from a process of study and discussion in the CSWE Community Organization Curriculum Development Project.[1] Another paper by Dr. Arnold Gurin considered broader curriculum issues in professional education for community organization practice.[2] While the material here will focus specifically on field instruction (or application training), reference to the broader issues raised elsewhere will be made as appropriate and useful.

---

[1] Publications resulting from the Community Organization Curriculum Development Project will be available soon. Tentative titles and publication dates are as follows: *Community Organization and Social Planning*, by Gurin and Perlman, and *Case Materials in Community Organization and Social Planning*, by Ecklein and Lauffer, in the spring of 1970; and *Community Organization Curriculum in Graduate Social Work Education: Report and Recommendations*, by Gurin, et. al., *Education for Application of Practice Skills in Community Organization and Social Planning: A New Look at Field Instruction*, by Rothman and Jones, and *Students in Schools of Social Work: A Study of Characteristics and Factors Affecting Career Choice and Practice Concentration*, by Goldman, Pins, and Jones, in the winter of 1969.

[2] Arnold Gurin, "Report on CSWE Community Organization Curriculum Development Project," paper presented at the CSWE Sixteenth Annual Program Meeting, Minneapolis, Minnesota, January, 1968.

JACK ROTHMAN is a professor at the University of Michigan School of Social Work and a member of the CSWE Community Organization Curriculum Development Project. This paper was originally presented at the Council on Social Work Education Sixteenth Annual Program Meeting in Minneapolis, Minnesota, January, 1968.

PROBLEMS OF FIELD INSTRUCTION IN
COMMUNITY ORGANIZATION

Our understanding of the current state of field instruction in community organization, including some of the more salient problems, is distilled from the results of an informal study, a later more structured one, writings in the literature, and an informed estimate based on personal observations and discussions with colleagues. The kinds of recommendations we will be making rely, in part, on this assessment of the current scene. Documentation has been offered elsewhere and will be specifically made in the final report. For the purposes of this presentation a brief sketch will suffice.

1. Change and growth in community organization in the schools, as well as in the field, have been marked and even dramatic. There has been a rapid build-up of a specialized student body (78 percent in one year), an increase in the number of schools offering two-year and one-year concentrations, and rising demands from the field for trained personnel.

2. Many of the new students are relatively young people with idealistic social change orientations and with experiences in a variety of "non-traditional" settings, such as Peace Corps, VISTA, the civil rights movement, OEO, SDS, and the like. Many of these students tend to be free-wheeling, problem- and social-action focused rather than profession focused, and critical of the social welfare establishment—that is, existing agency patterns and arrangements—as well as of the relevance of the academic program.

3. Schools are using a wide variety of new settings for placement and have gone far beyond the council of social agencies, the chest, and the settlement house. Students are placed in political organizations, militant civil rights groups, OEO programs, city planning commissions, governmental bureaus of all types at the city, county, regional, and national level, labor unions, civil liberties unions, etc. Most of the personnel in these newer settings have little or no familiarity with social work education or with social work itself. Traditional agency supervision is problematical or impossible in these situations. As Roland Warren has aptly described it, the practice context in and among agencies is "turbulent," or, in more cheery terms, "an exciting turmoil."[3]

4. There has been a "knowledge explosion" in the social sciences and professions which are associated with community organization—sociology, political science, social psychology, planning, etc. A much greater potential knowledge base exists to inform practice than has been the case heretofore. To varying degrees, this material is being incorporated into contemporary curricula.

---

[3] Roland Warren, "The Impact of New Design of Community Organization," *Child Welfare*, November, 1965, p. 495.

5. Many field instructors are not currently equipped with the newer knowledge and newer concepts which the schools are attempting to assimilate into their curricula. Our studies show that only 35 percent of all community organization field instructors have had formal preparation in community organization. A smaller percentage have had training in a contemporary program. Most field instructors have entered community organization through prior experience in casework or group work, and some have had no formal social work training. On the other side, few classroom teachers are experienced in dealing with rapidly changing problems and contexts in the field situation.

6. In the turbulent social situation in the world of practice, field instructors experience innumerable job pressures. Role strains develop between the production demands of the agency and the learning objectives of the school and student. For an agency practitioner, service goals have high saliency and one is expected to exhibit a high, or at least moderate, degree of loyalty to the objectives and programs of the agency. As a field instructor, one is expected to have a critical, objective, relativist stance regarding agency goals and methods. The practice-oriented person tends to *lean* toward development of skill and technique; the education-oriented person toward enhancement of theory and knowledge.

7. There is an inadequate experience base in community organization field instruction as compared to casework and group work. Conceptualization of objectives, assignments, supervision, recording, and so forth is still rudimentary and fragmentary in comparison with the more established methods in social work.

8. There is often concern over the problem of risk for the agency in terms of student performance. Because many of the student's functions are carried out in the public arena and outcomes are therefore visible, with far-reaching consequences for the community and agency (as well as for the student), administrators sometimes are reluctant to assign students to meaningful or sustained tasks or experiences.

9. There is considerable difficulty in defining a unit of work for placement purposes in community organization. There are few delimited, easily encompassable categories such as an individual client, a family, or a treatment group. Students may be assigned to one or more projects, committees, councils, studies, social problems, or the like, of varying intensity of activity and length of duration.

10. The pressures, irregularities, and fluidity of most community organization assignments make them difficult to locate in a standardized two- or three-days-a-week time schedule during an agency's program year. Students may not be on hand when situations ripen or events "pop." Developments race on between field days, and students have to be continually catching up. The student may consequently remain peripheral to the overall operations or culture of the agency.

11. Because of variations among settings and agencies (philosophy,

methods, structure), field instructors, client groups, stages of development in projects, and so forth, students have widely differing exposures in the field and consequently varied learnings. Schools have little operational control over what is learned, and, in most instances, cannot specify with even a moderate degree of exactness what students are actually learning in field agencies.

12. Perhaps one of the major problems is the discrepancy between what is learned in the classroom and what is learned in the field. There is reason to expect that one of the most serious existing problems is the lack of integration between academic and applied components of the educational regimen. For this reason, we will elaborate the discussion of this last problem area to a greater extent than the others.

In an informal, open-ended questionnaire study conducted by the Project in the spring of 1966, the most frequent evaluative comment by both students and field instructors had to do with the lack of integration between class and field. Field instructors indicated insufficient information about classroom subject matter and classroom teachers were often skeptical of certain practices and learning possibilities in the agencies. Some field instructors were critical of the amount and type of theory given in the classroom. Students, while recognizing the lack of fit, leaned either toward structuring their field experience to better test out theory, or seeking out areas of classroom content that might match more closely with the experiences and issues found in the field. Differences in intellectual backgrounds and outlooks of faculty and field instructors accounted in part for different emphases and lack of integration, but structural factors, such as physical distance between school and field, inadequate communication procedures between the two, differing functional demands in the two spheres of activity, etc., also contributed to this lack of integration. All in all, of the 73 students who responded to the open-ended questionnaire, 63 reported lack of integration between class and field.

Establishing a balance between academic work and application and the relative weights and interconnections between the two is probably the basic and most difficult problem in professional education. The following statement by G. Lester Anderson, a student of professional education, expresses the dilemma well.

Professional service rests on relative mastery of a relevant body of knowledge on the one hand and relative mastery of a professional craftsmanship on the other. What is the appropriate balance for the study of these two facets of professionalism? Forces exist which would push professional education now one way, now the other. The forces in the educational environment, most frequently, university forces, push for knowledge—knowledge which is derived from research and is rooted in and reinforced by theory. The forces emerging from practice push for craftsmanship or skill—the 'how we do it' which is practice. . . . The dualisms of knowledge vs. skill, theory vs. practice or basic vs. applied will probably be with us always. But these dualisms must be wrestled with continuously in professional education.[4]

GUIDING PRINCIPLES FOR FIELD INSTRUCTION OR APPLICATION TRAINING

Based on the foregoing assessment, the Project staff has arrived at certain principles for guiding a field instruction program, which, in our opinion, addresses some of these critical and recurring problems. The reader should keep in mind that the current first-year field format would be greatly affected by these new approaches, whereas the second-year format would not be very much affected.

1. *Integration of classroom teaching and application teaching.* To the greatest degree possible there should be a systematic, planned, and structured interrelationship of academic and application components of social work education. As stated in the more general curriculum paper:

> The key to our proposals in this area is the notion that there should be no teaching of methods and skills courses without field experiences built into the courses themselves, and conversely, that there should be no field experience which does not include a teaching seminar. In other words, we are suggesting that integration be achieved by looking at both the classroom work and the field instruction as courses, each designed to integrate knowledge and skills through experiences designed to provide specified learning experiences.[5]

2. *Diversification of teaching techniques and learning experiences.* It is short-sighted to be dependent on a single agency over an annual academic year for educational purposes. Students may learn practice skills through artificially structured campus-based means: role playing, simulation games, programmed learning experiences, computerized community problem-solving exercises, and the like. On the other hand, "real life" experiences can be partialized and delimited on a shorter- and longer-range basis in a variety of agency and community agency-free contexts in order to teach different concepts and skills (conducting a survey, engaging in a fund-raising campaign, planning and running a voter registration drive, etc.).

Returning to the broader curriculum paper, this idea is expressed as follows:

> In constructing the content of the methods courses, we are drawing again upon our description of practice, using the problem-solving model and

---

[4] G. Lester Anderson, "Professional Education: Present Status and Continuing Problems," in *Education for the Professions* (Chicago: National Society for the Study of Education, 1962).

[5] Gurin, *op. cit.*, p. 23.

the division of tasks into analytical and interactional elements. Courses are to include didactic material, observation, laboratory exercises, simulation, perhaps some experiments with programmed instruction, and discrete field experiences in agencies covering the range of direct organization, service, and planning and allocating which were outlined above. This means, for example, that students will be assigned to observe and participate in a study, or a problem-solving committee, or a budgeting process, or a fund-raising campaign, for a limited period of time, as an integral part of their class work in a methods course. This pattern will give students a broader range of experience in a variety of practice settings and will also enable the schools to use agencies and organizations in a more selective and defined manner for those experiences which they are best able to provide.[6]

This approach frees the student from the restricted exposure in experience, philosophy, or method embodied in any one agency. The student receives a comparative perspective and one that frees him to examine agency practice critically rather than forces him to become a captive of a particular agency orientation.

Because this more diversified approach to teaching practice skills breaks loose from placement in a single agency over an academic year, it might be well to make use of McGlothlin's term "application"[7] when referring to education in carrying out operationally the practice skills of the profession. This would include "field work" but also might entail skills exercises, planned observation of practice, laboratory tasks, etc. "Application training" implies a broader teaching technology than has been typically associated with "field instruction" in social work.

3. *Greater direction and control by the school of the educational experience for application training.* This implies greater faculty involvement in teaching skills and relating these skills to conceptual and theoretical constructs. Classroom faculty should structure tasks and exercises, monitor them, conduct seminars and other educational experiences, and in other ways become more closely identified with the process of teaching application skills. Through greater faculty participation, integration may be achieved more readily and new practice-related knowledge be conveyed to students in a fairly direct way.

4. *Specificity of learning objectives; explication of skills, relevant tasks and experiences.* In place of a rather global and diffuse approach to application training, we are recommending that schools be much more rigorous and exacting in selecting, from the vast array of all possible practitioner operations, that delimited and defined set of skills that they wish to convey to all students. In our final recommendations, we will be suggesting a laboratory section attached to methods courses

---

[6] *Ibid.,* p. 24.

[7] William J. McGlothlin, *The Professional Schools* (New York: The Center for Applied Research in Education, 1964).

as one way of accomplishing this and some of the other principles enunciated here.[8]

5. *Some rational, planned, and ordered sequencing of learning experiences.* In a previous paper, we suggested a scheme which would entail going from simpler to more complex tasks and contexts, from lower to higher levels of responsibility, from simulated experiences to actual practice functions.[9] One might reverse this and go from a global, full-exposure-to-the-world-of-practice experience to the conveying of more partialized sub-skills and conceptualizations. Which course one follows would depend, naturally, on the philosophy of education held and on assumptions about how students learn best. Confounding this problem is the consideration that different students learn best differently.

TWO AREAS OF LEARNING AND RELATED MODES OF TRAINING

It is the Project staff's view that there are two somewhat different (though related) kinds of learning that are necessary to developing competency in practice skill. One has to do with the acquistion of specific skills, such as community diagnosis, staffing committee meetings, preparing budgets, influencing community elites, interviewing a variety of different kinds of community actors, etc. The other is broader and not as easily defined or specified. It consists of: (1) exposure to a holistic experience in an agency—experiencing the agency as a total system, seeing the interconnections between one task and those of others in the agency, seeing the relationship of the agency and its program to other organizations and subsystems in the community, viewing the unfolding of multiple events and forces as they converge on the agency, and experiencing time pressures, multiple demands, and multiple role expec-

---

[8] It is interesting to note that the Project staff and the Tulane faculty working independently have arrived at certain similar conclusions. The Tulane approach is indicated below:

Standardizing content, learning experiences, and instruction so that all students had the opportunity to achieve a minimum basic core of learning; structuring objectives, content and learning experiences for sequence continuity and integration; integrating the content taught in class and field; achieving effective progression in the student's assumption of professional responsibility; integrating and balancing the intellectual and relationship components of the professional role; teaching the concept of 'agency' under conditions which minimized the individual agency apprenticeship influence.

Mary Lewis, *et. al., An Experimental Design for First Year Field Instruction* (New Orleans: Tulane Studies in Social Welfare, Tulane University, 1962).

[9] Jack Rothman, "Education for Professional Application: A Study of Field Instruction in Community Organization—A Interim Report," Community Organization Curriculum Development Project, Council on Social Work Education, August, 1966, pp. 67-70.

tations in the course of performing on the job; and (2) development of self-awareness and self-discipline in performing professionally. This means conscious attention to the use of the self as an instrument of change in a community context under circumstances of actual demands and tensions.

The Project is recommending that specific skills be acquired at an early point in the curriculum through a laboratory experience established in conjunction with the methods courses. Thus, each methods course would have associated with it a parallel practicum comprising specified tasks which involve operationalizing theories, concepts, and techniques taught in class as well as an opportunity for systematic observational analysis of phenomena associated with classroom teaching. The educational objectives related to application skills should be derived at every point from the content of academic teaching, primarily in the methods course. An analogue is the laboratory section of physical science courses such as chemistry or physics, where the lab section gives the student a chance to become involved behaviorally with theoretical content taught in a parallel time period—observing demonstrations and conducting experiments and other operations. A later, more sustained, and holistic experience, through ongoing responsibility in an agency, would permit the student to put these skills to work in actual practice conditions.

This format has the advantages of making a direct and inexorable link between class and field. It is necessary in constructing such an academic curriculum to take into account not only sequential academic learning but also aspects of concomitant application learning. Such academic or methods classes might be different in their design from those concerned with conceptual and theoretical content without deliberate relevance to application considerations.

A useful base for an initial methods course framework is the practice volume being produced by the Project. This volume contains many of the basic components for constructing a methods course with a concurrent laboratory-practicum experience either as a separate course or an application section of the methods course. The notion of analytical and interactional tasks suggests two different but related sets of practice skills. The problem solving steps and stages indicate specific implemental tasks to be mastered (of both an analytical and interactional nature). These tasks can be further differentiated and specified according to the three organizational settings in which they take place —direct organization of population groups, rendering direct services, and conducting planning and allocating functions.

In his overview curriculum paper, Dr. Gurin gave some examples of how this scheme fits together in terms of some actual practice situations.[10] I would like to expand these examples in order to illustrate more

---

[10] Gurin, *op. cit.*

concretely application training implications of the scheme. It was pointed out that, in the area of developing services, two aspects were important; one had to do with problem identification, the other with influence skills necessary to gaining acceptance of a given program. In the instance reported, a worker determined a need for legal service in a low-income area, but was unsuccessful in convincing the chairman of her board to enact the service. One set of largely analytical skills involved here is informal problem identification. A set of tasks to teach this material might be established as follows:

(Assume a laboratory neighborhood for a given team of students)

PROBLEM IDENTIFICATION

ANALYTICAL	*INTERACTIONAL*
Determining means of obtaining informal information from neighborhood residents regarding their needs.	Programmed instructional program in interviewing. Emphasis on establishing interview objectives.
Determining objectives of interviews, questions to be asked, interview process.	* * * * Informal interviews with public housing project residents regarding their needs.
Analysis of service data from community agencies.	Demonstration interview in classroom of an agency executive regarding use of services, by whom, gaps, and unserved populations. * * * * Obtaining service information and conducting service interviews with directors of community agencies— voluntary, public, police, employment, school principals, etc.
Analysis of demographic data.	Use of a simulation game on obtaining information. * * * * Interviewing selected personnel regarding availability, interpretation, and limitations of demographic data: City Planning Commission, Welfare Council, Research Department, Chamber of Commerce.

117

Analysis and interpretation of views of neighborhood leaders regarding neighborhood needs.

Planning a community meeting of neighborhood leaders regarding needs. Analysis of who should be invited (composition), legitimation, agenda, etc.

Interviewing heads of voluntary associations in laboratory neighborhood regarding need: civil rights groups, veterans associations, church groups, women's clubs, political parties, etc.

*   *   *   *

Making contacts to invite, conducting the meeting, making follow-up contacts.

INFLUENCE SKILLS

ANALYTICAL

Analysis of various modes of having recommendations accepted (advantages and disadvantages of each).

*   *   *   *

A list of possible alternatives is listed below.

*   *   *   *

Preparation of factual reports based on different strategies and publics.

INTERACTIONAL

Conduct a simulated staff meeting around diagnosing the problem.

Speak with chairman of board.

Role-play situation in class with different types of workers and chairmen and differing worker approaches.

Present findings to the entire board.

Students' presentation of findings of neighborhood survey to a local board.

*   *   *   *

Obtain tape recording of workers making recommendations to a board for analysis of behaviors at various stages.

Work with other board members.	Role play—board members having differing roles and interests.
Work through other community groups.	Student delivery of persuasive address in class. Critique by other students.
	* * * *
	Persuasive student address on study or other subject to selected neighborhood groups; other students as observers and critics.

The major implication of this laboratory strategy in further curriculum development in schools would be an effort to design academic content with explicit relevance to parallel skills-learning experiences. This strategy has great potential for redressing the current lack of integration between class and field.

Returning now to the more holistic experience, including self-awareness learnings, it is the view of the Project staff that these can be accomplished through a continuous placement in an on-going agency. This should involve an intensive experience carried out through a sustained responsibility over a period of time and should follow the initial skill development program. It is convenient to think of the skill development curriculum taking place in the first year and the holistic experience in the second. Block placement is probably the most advantageous way of achieving this objective, although concurrent placement may achieve the same objective in part. Block placement serves to correct some of the difficulties in concurrent agency placement mentioned earlier. In order to achieve a maximal educational impact including class-field integration, it is recommended that such sustained agency placements regularly have faculty-led seminars (in the field or in the school) built around them so that experiences, as they unfold naturalistically, can be analyzed and evaluated from the perspective of the broader intellectual orientation of the school.

FURTHER ASPECTS OF THE FIELD INSTRUCTION REPORT

We have suggested the general orientation and the framework of recommendations that will be contained in the final report on field instruction. Let us round this out with further details.

119

In terms of teaching specific skills through a laboratory-practicum arrangement, we intend to offer concrete tools and programs that can be used by schools. We will suggest an array of discrete, time-limited tasks and experiences in numerous agencies and in the community which can be brought together and packaged differently by different schools in order to teach skills. For that section of the report we will draw on activities along this line already being conducted in various forms in a number of schools. We are also exploring some of the newer educational technologies to see what they offer for special work application training, for example: simulation games, programmed learning possibilities, computerized learning techniques, and a range of other simulations, such as the in-basket technique, which has been used for training educational administrators. Before discussing the "holistic" aspect, it might be well to illustrate the character of discrete, time-limited experiences in community and agency by describing part of the program that was conducted at the University of California at Berkeley. This program seemed to incorporate to a considerable degree the approach to discrete, structured tasks and experiences envisioned by the Project staff.

Generally speaking, the Berkeley procedure involved students, under faculty direction, in a common core of similar experiences with a progression toward more active and responsible tasks. Tasks and educational objectives were determined on the basis of the faculty's judgment concerning skills required by a beginning practitioner for adequate performance. Educational objectives included an understanding of: (1) the urban community and its local neighborhoods; (2) the population and its social problems; (3) the operations and services of organizations (formal and informal), including social agencies; and (4) methods of intervention on the part of professional change agents. The first quarter gave attention to the community and its subsystems, including how agencies and organizations meet the needs of people. The second and third quarters were concerned with intervention, with an emphasis on organizing indigenous neighborhood groups to act on their own behalf. Students used as their organizational base service and training centers (community action service centers) operated by the School itself, but tasks involved agencies and groups located anywhere in the community. Experience in the first quarter included the following:

1. Observing and analyzing the intake process in a community action service center—observations taking place at the Center. Meeting with the worker to discuss nature of service, processes used, policies, and procedures. Going out with the worker on a community visit. Recording descriptively and analytically the observational experience. Learning objectives include an understanding of problems that bring people into contact with the social service systems, how these prob-

lems present themselves concretely, their effects on individual and family functioning, and the nature of services related to these problems, including eligibility and ineligibility for service. Interaction between worker and client also receives attention, including how problems are identified by the worker and how he fills a helping role. Aspects of the physical and social conditions in low income or minority urban neighborhoods also come into focus.

2. Serving as a social broker for families and/or individuals located in the course of the intake process. Providing social broker service for one to three cases located through intake. Interviewing and establishing working relationship with the client. Delineating services needed. Determining possible resources. Developing a plan of action, including priorities, in collaboration with the client. Accompanying and acting in behalf of the client in contacts with the social service system or other community institutions or groups. Educational objectives include developing skills in use of the advocate role and in establishing a helping relationship with a client, defining personal needs and sharing interviewing abilities, and also increased understanding of client problems and needs, and knowledge and effective utilization of the social service system.

3. Interviewing and observing the roles of selected professionals in major community institutions affecting neighborhood populations. Preparing a list of questions concerning role, function, and outlook of various neighborhood professional functionaries. Interviewing and observing in action: a public welfare social worker, a public health nurse, and a school principal. Also observing others from a list which includes community organizer, housing authority project manager, city planning department official, community relations police officer, etc. Writing up one interview as a process record, summarizing another more briefly. Learning objectives include skill in the formulation of questions to obtain information, interviewing, analysis of interview data, and disciplined observation of professional behavior, as well as knowledge of the roles and attitudes of allied professionals who affect neighborhood populations.

4. Observing key organizations and associations in urban communities. Visiting and observing at least one meeting in each of the following types of organizations: (1) governmental bodies—county board of supervisors, city or county planning commission concerned with housing, welfare, redevelopment, human relations, education; (2) voluntary agency board—YMCA, Girl Scouts, hospital, Red Cross; (3) OEO—governing board of a community action agency; (4) indigenous grass-roots organization in the students' selected neighborhood. Educational objectives include knowledge of the objectives, character, and programs of urban organizations, and acquisition of skill in observation and analysis of group process in task-oriented community groups.

5. Preparing a neighborhood profile, including basic data about the people, problems, organizations, and services in the neighborhood. Analyzing key problems and making suggestions about needed action. Educational objectives include skills in the collection of data, knowledge of neighborhoods conceived of as sub-community systems, and introduction to the use of community data in the formulation of goals and change strategies.

6. Participating in a voter registration campaign; visiting a designated number of neighborhood homes and registering a designated number of individuals. Educational objectives include the development of selected skills in neighborhood social action and knowledge of some aspects of the political and social action process.

Assignments in the third and fourth quarters involved students in common experiences involving a greater degree of personal responsibility. All students, working in teams, organized tenant organizations in public housing projects. Educational objectives focused on techniques of organizing low-income populations at the local level and the use of organizational structures and procedures, such as committees and other task groups. Knowledge of cultural patterns in a low-income population was given attention.

This Berkeley arrangement, the reader will note, incorporated a number of the "principles" previously suggested in this report, such as specification of core learning objectives and associated experiences for all students, greater faculty direction, etc. It does not appear sufficiently to treat the problem of integrating class and field learning.

In preparation for making recommendations concerning the more holistic, ongoing type of experience in an operating agency setting, we have conducted a survey of current field work patterns in agencies. This is the most extensive survey yet to have been conducted of field instruction in community organization. Replies were obtained from 422 community organization students in 21 schools of social work having appropriate concentrations. Data were also collected concerning field instructors and agencies.

In concluding this progress report, I would point out that the staff has seen the existence of the Project as an opportunity to take a fresh look at field instruction and to sketch out productive avenues of development unencumbered by tradition alone. Some of our recommendations will appear too radical to some social workers and educators, too conservative to others. We have attempted to hold an "objective" stance which makes a realistic assessment of existing problems in field instruction, and makes use of a variety of potential tools for developing the skills and competencies needed by the contemporary community practitioner.

PART IV
EVALUATION OF
STUDENT PERFORMANCE

ASSESSMENT OF STUDENT PERFORMANCE IN THE FIELD COURSE

NANCY KELLEY, MORTON PERLMUTTER,
AND G. VISWESWARAN

A STATEMENT of the philosophical stance of the School of Social Work
at the University of Wisconsin is required for full understanding of this
presentation. The most succinct statement of the School's position appears in Franks' paper:

> The philosophical approach of the school supports the idea of 'the
> autonomous social worker,' one whose knowledge, skill and understanding allows for work wherever a social worker is needed whether or not an
> appropriate agency exists. Most of our graduates do not have access to
> intensive supervision and consultation. This is true in corrections, where
> the probation officer is the court social worker in the county; the public
> assistance worker who, with a degree, is likely to be county director or
> supervisor of social services; the mental health worker who may be the
> social worker in a local mental health clinic or in a county mental hospital; the child welfare caseworker, group leader and community consultant. Many of our graduates soon become community and regional
> consultants in whatever field of interest. The School of Social Work seeks
> to produce a philosophy and to develop a curriculum to meet the needs
> of the State. However, the social work needs of the State are not essentially different from those of professional social work elsewhere.
>
> An essential characteristic of 'the autonomous social worker' is the
> ability to assume leadership in practice development and policy formulation. Our graduates now have many of the top positions in all aspects
> of social work in Wisconsin. We believe that our curriculum and pro-

NANCY KELLEY is a clinical instructor, MORTON PERLMUTTER an assistant professor, and G. VISWESWARAN a field work supervisor at the School
of Social Work of the University of Wisconsin in Madison. This paper was
originally presented at the Council on Social Work Education Sixteenth Annual Program Meeting in Minneapolis, Minnesota, January, 1968.

gram ought to be preparing the new generation of social work leaders. The basic position of the School of Social Work is severely generic. All students study and learn the methods of casework, group work, community organization and research. All students learn to understand social systems and then how to analyze them. Specificity of setting has reduced value in our curriculum.

Each time the term 'autonomous social worker' is used above it is in quotes, thus indicating that we realize that perhaps no social worker can ever be truly free and self-governing. We do think, however, that social workers can and must learn to be relatively unconstricted by traditional approaches to their task.[1]

Part of the school's orientation is the constant attempt to isolate the particular skill components inherent in what we have come to call "multi-method" practice. Rather than seek the elusive concept of integration of methodology, we are identifying the commonality of concept and theory basic to all social work practice. We are currently struggling with the problems of how, when, or whether to teach these commonalities in class or field. This is a complex problem since it appears to be less difficult to isolate and teach these components in the rarefied atmosphere of the academic classroom than in the pragmatically demanding environment of an agency. Yet, the opportunities for learning *in vivo* are more readily available in the field than in the classroom.

A brief review of these basic skill components is essential in order to clarify the kinds of expectations set up in both class and field courses. In the Social Work Methods sequence, students are presented with a concept of social work as "planned change" or a "problem-solving" process. The stages of the change process, based on a Lippitt model, are identified as:

Problem identification
Engagement with client system
Clarification of problem: definition of worker-client "contract"
Establishing goals for change
Working toward change
Generalization and stabilization of change
Termination with client system.[2]

In the first semester of the sequence, emphasis is placed on four groups of skills, which are necessary and relevant to social work practice with any client system—individual, group, or community. The first, and most basic, of these skill groups is *communication:* verbal, non-verbal; direct-indirect; information-giving, information eliciting,

[1] Virginia L. Franks, "The Autonomous Social Worker," *An Occasional Paper,* School of Social Work, University of Wisconsin—Madison, March, 1967.

[2] Ronald Lippitt, *et. al., Dynamics of Planned Change* (New York: Harcourt Brace and World, Inc., 1958).

and information reception. The second general grouping is identified as *data-collection skills*. Included in this unit of study (again, considering all client systems) are: sources of data, ways data are emitted, and ways in which data are sought, collected, and recorded. *Decision-making* skills are the third group; focus of study is on collation of data gathered, drawing inferences, and weighting of alternatives from available data. The fourth and final group of skills is called *intervention skills*. Here the effort is made to identify a broad range of role behaviors and to place them against different theoretical backgrounds and practice models for clarification and comparison.[3]

It is possible to see, from this brief summary, how these basic skill components can be developed into teaching goals for the field course. The field course is conceived to be a laboratory course in which the student is free, within the limits of competent and knowledgeable professional-academic guidance, to explore the applicability of skills to problems extant in clients or client groups.

This reference to the Social Work Methods sequence also supports our belief that the basic educational task of the school is to certify students to the social work profession. The diploma awarded to each student declares that he has acquired for himself a minimum degree of competence in the practice of social work. It is this responsibility for developing practice competence which leads us to support and give emphasis to the field course as a "laboratory." Since practice competence is our central objective in professional education, it follows that the educational experience must include opportunities for the student to practice, as well as to learn about, social work. We believe that field instruction is an integral part of the professional-degree program which produces the kind of practitioners in which we are interested.

Broad and ill-defined as the profession may presently be, we have drawn from it a range of settings for field practice and teaching. Approximately 200 students in the professional-degree program at Wisconsin complete field course requirements in 29 different field settings. The variety and number of field settings testifies, perhaps, to the comprehensive nature of the profession. This multiplicity of field settings allows the student to concentrate his efforts, during the second year, on the kind of experience which lends itself to his particular interest. Of the four semesters which are required in the field course, two are spent in each of two different placements. The second placement is, as far as possible, of the student's own choosing. In each placement, the student is required to have one or more direct experiences with an individual, a group, and a problem of community-wide concern.

During the past year, the significance of the student's experience in the field course has taken on special importance to us. This is reflected

[3] "Report of Ad Hoc Committee on Revision of First-Year Methods Course," School of Social Work, University of Wisconsin-Madison, April, 1967.

in a declared grading policy which stipulates that, if a student receives a grade of "C" in the field course, he cannot continue in the professional-degree program without faculty consent. The problem of giving a grade in the field course is a long-standing one. Because of the diversity of settings and the view of the field course as a laboratory in which the student increasingly integrates theoretical knowledge and practice ability, difficulties arise in determining the criteria for use in grading a student's performance. Approximately a year ago, we initiated the voluntary use of a field placement evaluation form. Though the form has not solved all the problems, it has served to focus the efforts of all field faculty around assessment of student performance in common areas.

Evaluation of student performance is made on a five-point scale:

1. Clearly below expected level
2. Below expected level
3. At expected level
4. Above expected level
5. Clearly above expected level

The areas in which evaluation is made are:

A. *Setting*
   1. Understands and uses policies and procedures of the setting.
   2. Identifies appropriately with the setting and its objectives.
   3. Uses knowledge of setting and community resources.
   4. Functions cooperatively with professionals and non-professionals.
   5. Organizes and plans his time and work.
B. *Practice*
   1. Develops constructive relationships which facilitate the helping process.
   2. Translates theoretical knowledge into practice.
   3. Applies knowledge of social systems and human behavior in the helping process.
   4. Engages himself in the active pursuit, coordination, and/or development of resources.
   5. Develops ability to gather and organize pertinent psycho-social-cultural data, to form appropriate judgments based on these, and to implement these at the practice level.
C. *Professional Self*
   1. Demonstrates conscious, disciplined use of self.
   2. Functions autonomously in areas of competence.
   3. Shows appropriate identification with the ethics and values of the social work profession.
D. *Supervision-Consultation*
   1. Recognizes and uses student role of learner.
   2. Uses help in transferring learning from one experience to another.

3. Uses supervisory help in evaluating practice.

E. In this setting, at this time, this student (is)   (is not) clearly suited for the profession of social work.

Signed: _____   _____

               Student   Field Instructor

Comments:[4]

Although the field evaluation form has identified for us the common areas in which all students have experiences in the field course, it has not presented any statement of standards for determining the level at which a student is presently performing. Basically, it is this question which has led to the development of the remainder of this paper. We have stated a view of the field course as a laboratory in which the student increasingly integrates theoretical knowledge and practice ability. The student brings into the field course the theoretical knowledge that he is developing from his classroom courses. The field instructor clearly has the responsibility for knowing the material that has been presented in class and for designing assignments in the field which will encourage the student to apply that knowledge. The field instructor must also develop and present content relevant to the specific field setting. The faculty member teaching in the field becomes something more than a "supervisor." Like other teaching faculty, he is responsible for development of teaching content (instruction) and for assessing the response of each student to that instruction.

Four areas stand out in defining the educational function of the field course. Each field setting must provide each student with the opportunity to concentrate on the following:

1. Concepts of social work as a profession and a growing identity as a member of it.

2. Knowledge about individuals, groups, communities, and social welfare institutions and systems.

3. Skills in communication, data-collection, decision-making, and intervention.

4. Behaviors which are consciously and selectively used to affect the goals which have been developed in a particular practice situation. (Defining the range of behaviors which a particular student has capacity for is perhaps the most difficult and evasive task that we have set for ourselves.)

Two things are implied in these four statements. One is that each student will bring to the educational experience his own background, professional interests, and capabilities. The business of professional education thus becomes highly individualized as the field instructor

---

[4] Field Placement Evaluation form of the Ad Hoc Committee on Evaluation, School of Social Work, University of Wisconsin, December, 1966.

works with each student to create an individual design for learning and professional development. The second implication is that it is, in fact, possible to state expectations for students in general as they move through the four semesters of the field course. We have begun to identify these progressive stages and to isolate the areas of concentration which seem to be appropriate to each. Our present system of assessing student performance relies heavily on the judgments of individual field instructors to determine whether a student is "at," "below," or "above" an expected level. The judgment factor cannot be eliminated, but we can try to generalize what it is he is making judgments about. The following statement of levels of expectation may or may not be unique; it is articulated for ourselves, for the profession, and for our students.

In considering the statement, keep in mind that the levels of expectation are viewed as progressive and somewhat sequential. It is also important to remember that each student will proceed at his own rate. Some will be ahead of a general expectation; others behind. Any one area of concentration may be a recurring goal to a particular student in each experience he has in the field course.

Levels of Expectation

(Areas in which student can be expected to concentrate)

1st Semester
generalized, exploratory

a. Student's perception of others.
b. Perception of self by others.
c. Perception of self as a "helping" person.
d. Observation, awareness, and identification of social problems and persons affected by them.
e. Concentration on communication and data-collection skills.
f. Identification of social work roles.

2nd Semester
specificity *re:* social problems

a. Development of conceptualizations: application of theory to observed problems.
b. Concentration on interpretation of data (decision-making skills).
c. Analysis and development of alternatives available to deal with observed problems (theoretical knowledge).
d. Alternative behaviors to be utilized in implementing (c) (Methodological knowledge).

a. Concentration of assignments which provide student with oppor-

130

3rd Semester specificity re: "practitioner" behaviors	tunities for practice of decision-making and intervention skills. b. Articulation by student of professional behavior to be utilized in carrying out an assignment re: a specific problem. c. Development of practice models which student can describe and use for problem-solving. d. Identification of social policy issues, administrative and social system implications of his experiences with people re: specific problems.

Levels of expectation for the second and third semesters may be viewed as interchangeable and are rather arbitrarily separated here. Some students learn more rapidly from the general to the specific (deductive reasoning, as outlined here in the sequence from second to third semester). Others will approach learning as inductive reasoning—from the specific experience to development of general principles.

4th Semester independent functioning with consultation	a. Integration by student of first three semesters' experience. b. Capacity to carry out with consistent productivity a variety of assignments. c. Defining limits and capacities for professional practice.

The application of this progression clearly helps the field instructor and the student develop highly specific expectations for a given semester's work. Furthermore, when the major areas of evaluation outlined previously are viewed from the general expectational level for a student in a given semester, they become sharper and much more definitive. An example may help to illustrate this point:

Student A, in the first semester of the field course, is assigned as co-worker in a treatment group of children. Selection of group members, development of individual treatment goals, design for development of the group, and confirmation of each child's participation will all be professional activities in which the student will be involved, but he will not have responsibility for final decisions in these areas. The group may, in fact, already be in existence with a defined number of members and already established modus operandi. The student's interest and assignments with the group can be expected to focus around questions of "How do these kids see me?" "What does this child's behavior mean to me, to himself, to other group members?" "What am I supposed to be doing with this group?" "Why did the other worker handle a situation as he did?" Though present and part of the situation, the student will, at the expected level, assume only limited professional tasks. His concentration will be very much on his perceptions of self, others, observed problems and behaviors, and appropriate social work roles. Similarly, a first-semester student assigned as the worker with an individual client will raise questions and concentrate his energies and efforts on developing an understanding of himself and his client, without making much progress toward effective intervention in the problems the client is experiencing. He may especially avoid dealing with emotionally laden content or hesitate to take initiative in the development and purposive use of a relationship.

Given the same assignment, *Student B,* in the third semester, will be expected to focus his efforts on:

- Formation of the group and carrying out all professional tasks which precede actual face-to-face contact with the group itself;
- Identifying and assessing patterns of social control, value systems, decision-making processes, inter-personal dynamics, individual responses to specific experiences, etc.;
- Selecting out those specific functions which the group does not perform well and specifying why the inter-personal system is not able to accomplish its goals;
- Studying alternatives by which he can bring about changes in the problematic areas and move the group toward accomplishment of its stated objectives; and
- Selecting, detailing, and carrying out the method which the student himself wants to use. (Here, the question of "range of behaviors" becomes evident again.)

An additional point should be made here. This particular example points up the differential learning that can take place in a field unit composed of students at all four semester levels of the field course. The first-semester student will get "feedback" from advanced students about himself, the questions he is focusing on, the assurance that they had similar experiences in their first-semester placements. He can see, in the experiences of students ahead of him, the more focused development to which his questions will lead. Similarly, students in the second, third, and fourth semesters may look back on and share their first experiences—though painful or naively perceived—with less self-protectiveness. The concentration of second- and third-semester students on conceptual models and their practice application can provide the base for assignments to all unit members for study and presentation for discussion of a particular model. The discussion that develops can provide rich opportunities for learning in seminar groupings.

Thus far we have traced the development of one school's approach to field teaching. At the University of Wisconsin, we have made a large investment in developing a philosophy and curriculum which stress initiative, creativity, and leadership in practice development. The question of defining levels of expectations in order to assess student performance in the field course has led to the development of a generalization, based on informal investigation, discussion with colleagues, and attempts to give some form to our beliefs and teaching styles. It appears from very recent discussion with the field teaching faculty in our school that this concept of levels of expectation will be useful in helping both the field instructor and individual student in determining his performance level: whether "below," "at," or "above" expectation. Clearly, the student whose predominant pattern of performance is "at" the expected level is a B student.

In order to be useful, this standardized statement of levels of expectation requires some translation in its use with each student. Initially, the field instructor must "translate" the educational goals and philosophy of the School into the context of the particular field setting. As assignments are developed, those assignments must be "translated" into progressive goals for continued learning. Finally and continuingly, the field instructor must "translate" the experiences and assignments in the particular field setting back into the general framework for evaluation of the student's performance.

"Feedback" from students suggests that experiences in the field course are most meaningful and clear when a highly specific assignment is made, when the student understands what he is expected to do with the assignment, and when he has an opportunity to review his performance with the field instructor. Some examples of these assignments are: interviewing a number of people, recording and reporting the information which has been gathered, evaluating the data, arriving at a decision about the nature of the problems which the data supports, determining specific things the student can do about the problem, and carrying out the specific plan with the client. Each of these specific pieces of activity could be viewed as a separate assignment geared toward developing the student's "ability to gather and organize pertinent psycho-social-cultural data, form appropriate judgments based on these, and implement these at the practice level." Each of the items on the Field Course Evaluation form can lend itself to the same kind of specificity.

Specificity seems to be the key to this concept of field teaching. Clearly defined and bounded assignments, clearly stated and understood expectations, and projected goals from one stage of learning and demonstrated ability to the next all impose on the field instructor the responsibility for translating from the general to the specific with each student—and back again. The conceptual model of levels of expectation developed earlier in the paper represents no more than an intentionally designed series of specifics.

Having come this far, there are questions which have not been answered. The direction of this paper strongly suggests that relying on the "practice wisdom" of field instructors will not be sufficient if we are trying to factor out the discrete variables that go into professional education. We have concentrated on attempting to standardize those areas in which all students are expected to have practice experience. This attempt at standardization is represented in the Field Course Evaluation form. As we continue to use it, it may provide more accurate information about the areas in which field instructors make key judgments about student performance.

The relationship between the field course and the Social Work Methods sequence is evident. Can the same correlation be developed between the Field Course and the other sequences—namely, Human Behavior and Social Environment, Social Policy and Administration, and Methods of Social Work Research? If specificity is a key principle in field teaching, what kinds of thing does the field instructor do to produce clearly defined learning experiences? This paper further suggests that determining the level at which a student is expected to perform and assessing that performance in the field course is primarily the responsibility of the field instructor and the student. What about the expectations of host agencies which provide the settings for much of our field instruction? Is there a conflict between the heavy emphasis suggested here on learning and limited performance and the expectations which an agency may have for carrying a caseload, getting the work done, producing results?

The material developed and presented in this paper and the unanswered questions which have been raised all need to be subjected to carefully developed research inquiries. As with "practice wisdom," we need to dissect the whole into those finite pieces which make up field instruction. Clarification of what we mean by "professional education" in social work is dependent on it.

MEASURING STUDENT PERCEPTION OF FIELD INSTRUCTION

SHELDON D. ROSE, JANE LOWENSTEIN, AND PHILLIP FELLIN

EFFORTS ON THE PART of educators and practitioners are increasingly being devoted to the description, evaluation, and development of the practice skill component of social work education. New models of field instruction utilize both campus and agency-based instruction, increase opportunities for integration of field experience and classroom teaching, and concentrate on sequential learning. These developments have stimulated new approaches for measurement of the student's learning and performance in practice tasks. Generally, the source of information has been the field instructor and/or a representative from a school of social work.[1] A somewhat neglected source of information about the practice skill experience is the student himself. Tapping both instructors and students for information can lead to a comprehensive picture of the student's skill training, indicate various strengths and limitations in current patterns of field instruction, and suggest possible guidelines for change.

Systematic study of the student's view of his field experience calls for the design and testing of appropriate evaluation instruments. A significant effort in this direction is the Relationship Scale developed by Rose in a research study of students attending the Social Academy in

---

[1] For a survey of relevant studies, see Merlin Taber, "A Sampling of Techniques for Evaluative Research in Field Instruction," *Social Work Education Reporter* Vol. 15, No. 3 (September, 1967), pp. 22 ff.

At the time this paper was written, SHELDON D. ROSE was a professor at the University of Michigan School of Social Work. He is now deputy director of the Peace Corps in Nepal. PHILLIP FELLIN is a professor and JANE LOWENSTEIN an associate professor at the University of Michigan School of Social Work.

Appreciation is expressed to Elizabeth Navarre, Esther Sales, Kate Grenholm, John Riley, and Thomas Powell for their helpful comments on the paper.

Amsterdam, the Netherlands.[2] The present paper describes an extension of the Dutch study, presents a refined measurement instrument, and reports data collected in use of the instrument with students from the University of Michigan School of Social Work.

CONCEPTUAL FRAMEWORK

The conceptual framework for this study was derived from the research by Rose on students engaged in field work experience in the Netherlands. The principal hypothesis of the Dutch study predicted that the intensity of a student's criticism of his field instruction experience is, in part, a function of the level of learning which the student has attained, i.e., beginning students were expected to be more critical than more advanced students. The rationale for this prediction was based on the assumption that the new student in a field placement is under pressure to act in relation to a set of performance criteria with which he cannot yet conform. In such a demanding situation, the student is likely to project responsibility for his predicament onto the field instructor. As time passes and the student gains in knowledge and skill, he is better able to meet performance demands for service to clients and, as a result, becomes less critical of the behavior of his field instructor. The data of the study support this proposition. In this paper, the hypothesis is examined with data from students in an American school of social work.

A second hypothesis examined in the current study is concerned with selected areas of supervisory activities. Areas relevant to the student's evaluation of his practice skill learning include cognitive-structuring, emotional support, and autonomy-giving. *Cognitive-structuring* refers to actions by the field instructor which provide the student with information and other intellectual resources necessary to clarify and/or structure the work situation, or to facilitate the application of theory to practice. *Emotional support* refers to actions by the field instructor which encourage the expression of student attitudes and feelings, demonstrate attitudes, and reward correct or appropriate performance. *Autonomy-giving* refers to actions by the field instructor which facilitate the student's performance of decision-making activities and enhance his independent functioning. It is hypothesized that students perceive their field instructors as providing less, or less adequate, cognitive structure than emotional support of autonomy. This is suggested by the findings of the Dutch study and by social work literature concerning supervision, which deals mostly with emotional support and autonomy-giving attitudes of supervisors. Less attention is given to techniques or procedures for structuring the work situation or teaching the student.

In addition to our examination of two hypotheses, we explore the

---

[2] Sheldon D. Rose, "Students View Their Supervision: A Scale Analysis," *Social Work*, Vol. 10, No. 2 (April, 1965), pp. 90-96.

relationship of student perception of field instruction to method of practice (casework, group work), type of instruction (individual, group), sex of student and instructor, and field instruction grade.

RESEARCH DESIGN

Students at three different stages in their social work education were included in the study: those completing the first semester of classroom work and field experience; those completing the second semester; and those completing the fourth semester.[3] The fourth-semester students had been exposed to two different field placement agencies; the first- and second-semester students to only one. Only students with placements in casework, group work, or a combination of the two were included in the study. The instrument items were not considered to be fully appropriate for other specializations such as community practice or administration.

A total of 346 students, all attending a single school of social work, comprised the student population for the study. Utilizing a combination of classroom handouts and mailings, we obtained responses from 261 students (75.4 percent). The response rate for various sub-groups (casework and group work; first- and second-year students) varied little from the overall response rate. Thus, the non-respondents were similar to the respondents along at least the two dimensions of phase of learning and method of practice.

The reactions of students to their field instruction were obtained at a single point in time. This aspect of the design is somewhat limiting; it is possible that systematic differences among students in different phases of the program could account for differences in the kind of perceptions obtained. Several possible sources of such differences might include: (a) shifting criteria for admission to the school; (b) recent attraction of new types of people to the field of social work; (c) objective differences in the quality of the field instructors involved with students in the different phases; and (d) varied strength of group norms legitimating critical opinions of field instruction. A longitudinal study, measuring the reactions of the same students to the same instructors at different points in time, would allow for control of some of these factors and lead to a more accurate picture of the effect of phase of learning on the tendency of a student to view field instruction in a particular way.

THE RESEARCH INSTRUMENT

Students' perceptions of field instruction were measured through a questionnaire containing 25 statements concerning various specific ac-

---

[3] Data were obtained at the completion of the 1966-67 academic year, a time at which there were no third-term students in attendance at the school.

tivities of a field instructor. An example of an item formulated to measure the emotional support (ES) dimension is, "When I am somewhat 'down,' he helps me to build my enthusiasm for the work." An example of a cognitive-structuring (CS) item is, "He helps me evaluate the degree to which treatment goals are being achieved." An autonomy-giving (AG) item is, "He lets me discover my own errors." For each statement, the student was asked to specify the frequency with which his instructor engaged in that particular behavior. The student also indicated what he perceived to be the ideal frequency for that behavior. The following example illustrates the way in which the response choices were structured. A six-point scale was employed: always (A); almost always (AA); usually or frequently (UF); seldom (S); rarely (R); and never (N).

ILLUSTRATION I

He helps me to evaluate the degree to which treatment goals are being achieved.

Actual	☐	☐	☐	☒	☐	☐
	A	AA	UF	S	R	N
Ideal	☐	☐	☐	☐	☐	☐
	A	AA	UF	S	R	N
	(1)	(2)	(3)	(4)	(5)	(6)

If a student felt that his instructor sometimes helped him evaluate the degree to which treatment goals were being achieved (4), but felt that a field instructor should ideally do this always (1), a discrepancy of three units (4-1) was designated as the student's response to that item.

The discrepancy between the actual and ideal frequencies for a particular item was taken as an indication of the student's evaluation of his instructor's performance for that item. In computing this discrepancy, we were interested in the absolute magnitude of the difference between the actual and ideal frequencies, not in the direction of the discrepancy.

The sum of the discrepancies between actual and ideal behaviors for all 25 items was considered a measure of the extent of the student's total evaluation of his field instructor. The underlying assumption is that the 25 items are a representative sample of the universe of the field instructor's student-related behavior. The sum of these discrepancies was designated as the student's Actual-Ideal Discrepancy (A.I.D.) Score. The magnitude of the A.I.D. scores allows for a comparison of individual students or groups of students in terms of their evaluation of their field instructors.

Nine faculty members evaluated the 25 items in terms of their dimensions, reaching sufficient agreement on ten items as measures of CS, eight items as measures of ES, and five items as measures of AG. The remaining two items were not used in the sub-scales, as there was insufficient agreement regarding the predominant dimensions to which they belonged. These items were included, however, in the total A.I.D. scores, since they apparently tapped aspects of several dimensions and were generally perceived to be "highly relevant" items by the judges.[4] Sub-scale scores were obtained by adding the discrepancies for the items included in each of the three dimensions and then dividing by the number of items in the given dimension. The sub-scale scores served as a means of comparing the student's evaluation of his field instructor in each of the three areas. For example, if one student had a CS score of 1.4, an ES score of 1.0, and an AG score of .8, we would say that he perceived the most discrepancy in his instructor's cognitive-structuring behaviors and the least discrepancy in his autonomy-giving behaviors.

SELECTED FINDINGS

Hypotheses. The first hypothesis predicted an inverse relationship between the extent of the student's criticism of his field experience and the phase of learning in which the student was involved; that is, beginning students were expected to be more critical than advanced students. This hypothesis is not supported by our data. A comparison of the A.I.D. scores shows that first-semester students have a lower mean A.I.D. score than second-semester students; both groups have lower scores than fourth-semester students. Thus, with increasing experience and knowledge, students are found to perceive more, rather than less, discrepancy between the actual and ideal behaviors of field instructors. The trend of increased magnitude was found for the total A.I.D. scores as well as for each of the three sub-scales. These findings are summarized in Table 1.

Our second hypothesis predicted that students would perceive greater discrepancy between actual and ideal behaviors in cognitive-structuring than in emotional support or autonomy-giving. Data in Table 1 show support for this hypothesis, with a consistent rank order among the three dimensions; each semester A.I.D. scores are highest for cognitive-structuring items and lowest for autonomy-giving items.

In order to determine whether or not these findings hold for both case-

---

[4] The judges were asked to place each item in one of three sub-scales. If a judge thought that an item belonged in two or more sub-scales, he was to indicate into which category an item most nearly overlapped. He could also indicate a second choice as well. An item was included in a given sub-scale if at least six of the nine judges considered it belonged primarily to that sub-scale, and at least one of the remaining judges indicated that it belonged secondarily to that sub-scale. The judges were also asked to judge the relevance of all items. An item was included in total A.I.D. test if eight out of the nine judges ranked it as relevant or highly relevant. Items not used in sub-scales were: "He lets me know exactly how he perceives I am doing." "When I have work patterns which interfere with my effectiveness he helps me to perceive them."

TABLE 1

Mean A.I.D. Scores by Semesters Completed

Supervisory Activities	Semester			All Respondents (N=257)
	First (N=42)	Second (N=105)	Fourth (N=110)	
Autonomy-Giving	.85	.93	1.07	.98
Emotional Support	.87	1.14	1.25	1.14
Cognitive-Structuring	1.27	1.34	1.48	1.39
Total Test	1.07	1.22	1.32	1.24

work and group work students, we examined the hypotheses using method of practice as a control variable. Table 2 indicates that, for casework students, the total A.I.D. and sub-scale scores increase with increased time in field instruction, for example, for autonomy-giving, .87 compared to 1.09. Thus, the obverse of the first hypothesis holds for casework students. For group work students, no clear-cut patterns are obtained.

TABLE 2

Mean A.I.D. Scores by Practice Method and Semesters Completed

Supervisory Activities	Casework				Group Work			
	Semester				Semester			
	1	2	4	All	1	2	4	All
	(N=25)	(N=75)	(N=72)	(N=172)	(N=15)	(N=28)	(N=35)	(N=78)
Autonomy-Giving	.87	.95	1.09	.99	.88	.91	.92	.91
Emotional Support	.83	1.12	1.26	1.13	.95	1.21	1.10	1.12
Cognitive-Structuring	1.23	1.36	1.52	1.41	1.40	1.30	1.29	1.32
Total Test	1.04	1.23	1.35	1.25	1.16	1.22	1.15	1.18

In summary, data in Table 1 show no support for the hypothesis in the Dutch study that intensity of criticism decreases with each level of learning. By contrast, a definite increase in intensity of criticism with each semester of learning is found. However, when the data are controlled by method of practice, only for casework students does criticism increase with each phase of learning. Table 2 also indicates that casework students are slightly more critical than group work students in two of the areas of supervisory behaviors. One explanation for these findings concerns the extent to which a knowledge gap exists between field instructors and the school. As the student progresses through his educational program, classroom learning tends to clarify what he should be doing and learning in the field experience, and to reveal any gaps between school and field. As gaps are uncovered, the student is likely to become more critical of his instructors' behavior, especially in cognitive-structuring. Why, then, does criticism not increase by semester for group work students? Perhaps there are fewer gaps between the group work classroom and field teaching.

Type of Supervision. In addition to examining the two study hypotheses, we were interested in exploring the way in which A.I.D. scores are related to the type of student supervision. While the major portion of students (215) in the study received individual supervision, a small number of students (35) received either group supervision or a combination of individual and group supervision. Students with individual supervision were found to have lower mean A.I.D. scores for each of the three dimensions than the group supervision students. Thus, as Table 3 indicates, students with individual supervision perceive less discrepancy between the instructor's actual and ideal behaviors than do students with group supervision.

TABLE 3

Mean A.I.D. Scores by Type of Supervision

Supervisory Activities	Individual Supervision (N=215)	Group Supervision (N=35)
Autonomy-Giving	.95	1.10
Emotional Support	1.07	1.39
Cognitive-Structuring	1.33	1.57
Total Test	1.18	1.44

The tendency of students receiving individual supervision to be less critical of the instructor's behavior continues to hold when the findings are controlled by phase of learning.[5] However, when practice method is introduced as a control variable, casework students receiving some group supervision have approximately the same mean A.I.D. scores as do students with individual supervision. It is only among group work students that the findings are in the direction of lower A.I.D. scores accompanying individual supervision; that is, for group work students, there is much greater criticism of group supervision than of individual supervision (Table 4).

In the light of the assumptions currently made about group supervision, we were surprised to discover that, among group workers, group supervision received greater criticism (higher A.I.D. scores) than individual supervision. One could expect that group work field instructors

---

[5] Data available from the authors but not included in the text.

141

TABLE 4

Mean A.I.D. Scores by Method and Type of Supervision

Supervision	Casework (N=172)	Group Work (N=78)
Individual	1.36	1.16
Group	1.35	1.64

would be particularly skillful in the use of the group as the context and means of supervision. Our findings may be due, in part, to deficiencies in the kind of group supervision given at the time of the study, as well as to the fact that, in some situations, the field instruction was a mixture of group and individual instruction. Also, the measurement items may be more appropriate to the individual model of field instruction.

Differences by Sex. In exploring the influence of the sex of student and the field instructor on the student's view of his supervision we found no significant pattern of differences. Male students perceived slightly less discrepancy than female students between the instructor's actual and ideal behaviors. The sex of the student and field instructor were considered in relation to autonomy-giving, emotional support, and cognitive-structuring as follows: (1) male students with female instructors; (2) male students with male instructors; (3) female students with female instructors; (4) female students with male instructors. The differences between groups are extremely small and not consistent over the three sub-scales.

Field Instruction Grade. For some students (second and fourth semester), it was possible to explore the relationship between the student's evaluation of field instruction and the grade received for the prior semester's field work (in the same agency and with the same field instructor). Table 5 indicates that, with one exception, the lower the grade received, the higher the mean A.I.D. scores for each of the dimensions. The exception occurs in the lowest reported grade category (B— or lower), which included only ten students for whom the range of the scores was large.

At least two interpretations can be made about our findings concerning the relationship of grades to A.I.D. score. Students who have been rewarded with high grades by their field instructors may in turn reward their instructors by perceiving little discrepancy between the instructor's actual and ideal behaviors. In addition, students who receive high field instruction grades may be receiving "better" field instruction as reflected in the smaller A.I.D. scores. A comparison between students with the same field instructor would be necessary to determine which of these factors is most relevant in accounting for the observed relationship between grades and A.I.D. scores.

142

TABLE 5

Mean A.I.D. Scores by Field Instruction Grade and Supervisory Activities

Supervisory Activities	Grade				
	A (N=25)	A— (N=54)	B+ (N=84)	B (N=45)	B— or lower (N=10)
Autonomy-Giving	.66	.91	1.04	1.31	1.14
Emotional Support	.74	.98	1.28	1.61	1.18
Cognitive-Structuring	1.05	1.32	1.47	1.67	1.47
Total Test	.87	1.13	1.33	1.60	1.39

CONCLUSION AND IMPLICATIONS

In this study we have sought to demonstrate the usefulness of an instrument designed to measure student perception of field instruction. Data so obtained can provide some direction for the school's effort in the development and improvement of field instruction. For example, attention could be given to the cognitive-structuring area in school-agency contacts. This could be achieved by means of faculty-liaison field instructor discussions, school-sponsored meetings for agency field instructors, seminars on supervision, and manuals and instructional materials provided by the school.

A second major finding of the study shows a lack of support for the proposition that the intensity of criticism of field instructors' behaviors will decrease with each level of learning. In fact, for casework students, a clear trend of increased criticism is found with each additional semester. On the other hand, no clear pattern emerges for group work students. It is interesting to note, however, that criticism in the area of cognitive-structuring is found to be the lowest in the final (fourth) semester for group work students and highest in this semester for case-work students. The data suggest that differential efforts in working with casework and group work field instructors, as well as with instructors for first- and second-year students may be needed.

Our data have allowed us to examine the relationship of selected factors to student perception of field instruction, thereby suggesting implications for introducing changes into classroom and field teaching. At the same time, we would emphasize the fact that a complete evaluation of practice-skill learning requires information from additional sources, especially from field instructors, classroom instructors, educational coordinators, and faculty liaison to agencies and agency executives. When adequate and valid information is obtained, general patterns of field instructors' behaviors and student performances can be assessed and utilized by a school, in addition to reference to specific student-field instructor relationships.[6]

[6] Scale items for the dimensions of Autonomy-Giving, Emotional-Support, and Cognitive-Structuring are listed below. For each dimension, the items are ordered in terms of mean Actual-Ideal discrepancy scores found in this study (from low to high). For the questionnaire, the items were distributed randomly.

I. *Autonomy-Giving*
   1. He encourages me to try to solve my own problems with clients.
   2. He lets me discover my own errors.
   3. The content of conferences is basically what I determine it to be.
   4. When I have original ideas, he encourages me to experiment with them.
   5. He helps me to develop my own learning goals.

II. *Emotional Support*
   1. He shows interest and concern in my progress.
   2. He acknowledges my perception of the bases of any difficulties I may have with clients.
   3. He acknowledges all actions which I perceive I've done well.
   4. When I am concerned or anxious about new situations, he helps me to deal with these feelings.
   5. When I am somewhat "down" he helps me to build my enthusiasm for the work.
   6. He demonstrates clearly by his behavior with me how I should act with others.
   7. When I disagree with him, he encourages me by his actions as well as his words to express it.
   8. When I am dissatisfied with some aspect of field instruction, he encourages me to talk about it.

III. *Cognitive-Structuring*
   1. He helps me to take into account the client's individual psychological factors which affect the treatment process.
   2. He helps me to consider agency practices which influence the treatment process.
   3. He helps me to establish treatment goals for clients.
   4. He helps me to take into account societal factors which impinge upon the treatment process.
   5. As I need them, he suggests specific intervention techniques.
   6. He helps me to apply theoretical concepts in the analysis of my practice.
   7. He assists me in systematically structuring my own thinking in the problem areas where I am not clear.
   8. He helps me to take into account the small group factors which affect the treatment process.
   9. He helps to clarify all tasks expected of me in my field placement.
   10. He helps me to evaluate the degree to which treatment goals are being achieved.

PART V
ADMINISTRATION OF
FIELD INSTRUCTION

ROLE AND FUNCTION OF THE COORDINATOR OR DIRECTOR OF FIELD INSTRUCTION

HELEN CASSIDY

INTRODUCTION

In order to define the role and responsibilities of the director or co-ordinator of field instruction, it is essential to state the basic assumptions that the school holds about curriculum and to clarify the place and definition of field instruction within the curriculum. An authority in the area of field instruction admonishes that "a distinction should be made between fundamental policy decisions—choices that govern the direction of the field work course—and operational decisions that are logically subsidiary."[1] One might elaborate the statement to indicate that these operational decisions are not only subsidiary to but actually an outgrowth of the policy decisions. Hence, the role of coordinator of field instruction is not a prescribed, static role which is self-explanatory. It is a role which carries many possibilities and demands as to responsibility, coverage, and function.

The differences in role execution are many if one is to do a comparative analysis. The mutations within the role in one school will vary greatly over a time span as the conception and expectations of the role expand or constrict, become responsive to new trends, and seek to chart new ways of performing. Depending on the focus of the job, one may

---

[1] Margaret Schubert, "Curriculum Policy Dilemmas in Field Instruction," *Journal of Education for Social Work*, Vol. 1, No. 2 (Fall, 1965), p. 36.

HELEN CASSIDY is coordinator of field instruction at the Tulane University School of Social Work. This paper was originally presented at the Council on Social Work Education Sixteenth Annual Program Meeting in Minneapolis, Minnesota, January, 1968.

describe the behavior of the role bearer as: trouble-shooter with agencies; super "con" artist who extracts additional student placements from hard-pressed agencies; manipulator of placements trying to "make do" in reconciling the student population with agency offerings, however disparate; consultant helping agency instructors to approach integration of class content with field performance; educational coordinator seeking to tie together and move forward a total operation with school-based educators committed to a common body of material, specifically defined and sequentially ordered. I submit that the behavior of the coordinator of field instruction is more than likely a mixture of several of these job descriptions with primary weight falling in one or two areas.

In this paper, I will attempt to show that the role definition of coordinator of field instruction derives from the concept of curriculum held by the school, and I will cite the experience of the Tulane School of Social Work to prove the thesis.

ASSUMPTIONS ABOUT FIELD INSTRUCTION

Fundamental to all of our thinking and changes at Tulane are the following tenets which we hold about field instruction:

- That field instruction is an integral part of the curriculum;
- That field instruction is a sequence in its own right with a body of material to be taught;
- That field instruction is that section of the curriculum where the availability of sense data supplies the appropriate environment for testing theoretical formulations;
- That field instruction supplies that mode of learning essential to any professional school—making knowledge available for use; and
- That field instruction serves as a crossroads where new ideas and theoretical formulations about practice can be tested for their efficacy in relation to contemporary and future social work jobs.[2]

At the second level of generalization, we believe that the following specific objectives of field instruction must be addressed:

Standardizing content, learning experiences, and instructions so that all students have the opportunity to achieve the minimum basic core of learning.

Structuring objectives, content, and learning experiences for sequence, continuity, and integration.

Teaching major concepts of all curriculum areas in the field instruction context.

Integrating the content part in class and field.

---

[2] ". . . each system of education must face the upsetting question of whether it wants its students to be trained for a profession as it was and is or as it should be and might become." Henry David, "Education for the Professions: Common Issues, Problems, and Prospects," *Journal of Education for Social Work,* Vol. 3, No. 1 (Spring, 1967), p. 10.

Achieving effective progression of professional responsibility.

Obtaining and developing student initiative, creativity, and independence.

Integrating and balancing the intellectual and relationship components of the professional role.

Teaching the concept of "agency" under conditions which minimize individual agency apprenticeship influences.[3]

Preparing students for social work job demands which introduce them to social work as a field of practice and equipping them with the capability of practicing within at least two of the instrumental technologies (casework, group work, community social work, etc.) at a major and minor level of beginning competence and with broad acquaintance with the other phases of practice.

In the past nine years, the field curriculum at Tulane has undergone marked changes as the total curriculum has been revised. I will attempt to show this evolving process by giving a brief historical sketch, the current curriculum picture with particular emphasis on field instruction as an integral part, the place of the faculty field instructor as social work educator, and the type of field learning environment devised to implement curriculum goals.

HISTORICAL PERSPECTIVE ON THE CHANGE

A brief historical reflection will help to put our present scheme into perspective. Dissatisfaction with the educational aspects of field instruction led the Tulane faculty to experiment with a structure that might afford better curriculum planning, take into account the needs of graduate students as adult learners, and give cognizance to an approach that would make assumption of professional responsibility commensurate with readiness to perform. Research to explore these propositions was carried out in 1959-60. Emphasis in this experimental structure was to provide students with a degree of security that would help them to integrate the total curriculum of the school and provide "a continuous rapprochement of learning objectives, learning experiences, learning tasks, and learning needs of the individual student."[4]

Peer learning added a dimension of enrichment that made the student more responsible for his own learning and point of view—a significant factor in advancing the attributes of the adult learner. This form of pedagogy simultaneously diluted the intensity of the student's relationship to the field teacher who, within this learning environment, more realistically assumed the role of instructor.

---

[3] Mary Lewis, Dorothy Howerton, and Walter Kindelsperger, *An Experimental Design for First Year Field Instruction* (New Orleans: School of Social Work, Tulane University, 1962), pp. 7-8.

[4] *Ibid.,* p. 26.

SOME ASPECTS OF CURRICULUM REVISION

The results of this initial research freed the school to engage in other pursuits of an exploratory nature. Shortly after the year of experimentation in the field, the faculty, with an awareness of the importance of seeking an end product that would link and integrate class and field curriculum content into a unified whole, began a revision of the curriculum. Emphasis was placed on effecting a continuum within the curriculum that reflected continuity and sequential development, not only on a horizontal plane (the student's longitudinal development) but also on the vertical level, where the goal was integration of all courses and practice experience at specific phases in the student's learning. Class work was related more closely to field experience. Field instruction content development, subjected to the same rigorous discipline as the class content, became a fully respectable component of the curriculum.

The approach to total curriculum revision was one of research and demonstration of feasibility. Each part of the class content was tested before any final revision was made. The same was true with field instruction. The changes were effected by a process of sample testing rather than by any one major change at a given time.

THE FACULTY FIELD INSTRUCTOR AS EDUCATOR

Our convictions about curriculum and how it should be taught, especially in the first year, led to the decision to employ a corps of faculty-appointed field instructors—a group of educators whose complete commitment was to teaching in the field. The attendant thinking, exploration, evaluation, and sharing among faculty colleagues of the classroom and the field in uncharted areas of structured teaching in the field has had an impact upon the total curriculum.

Faculty share common concerns and assume joint responsibilities for utilizing the interrelationship of these two learning modes. No longer do classroom teachers appropriate the sole right to set the overall pace for content presentation with the onus on the field teacher to make sure students "are getting it" in practice placements. Field instructors, for their part, with a new sense of clarity and purpose about the dimension of their task, are able to identify flaws in timing in classroom presentation of material. This criticism eventually brings about alterations in the timing sequence in class. By working together on curriculum planning committees, these respective teachers make joint decisions about material to be taught and the timing. Participation of some field instructors in classroom teaching rounds out the process of planning, exchange, mutual decision, and integration.

For three years now, all first-year field instruction has been carried out by faculty appointees. Approximately 80 percent of the second-year students receive faculty field instruction.

At the time that we moved toward employing full-time educators for the field, there were other converging forces with which we were required to reckon. The upsurge in enrollment and the inability of agencies to accommodate growing demands for space and the use of their personnel for instructional purposes were noteworthy among them. Such considerations were supportive but not decisive in the commitment to employ faculty-based educators for field instruction. The field curriculum, as we saw it, called for persons who could bring to the assignment the time, capacity, investment, and sense of inquiry necessary to do a comprehensive teaching job.

THE TRAINING CENTER AS FIELD LEARNING SETTING[5]

A variety of pressures and stimuli moved the school to the development of the training center as an ideal learning environment. The critical situation in agencies which precluded additional pre-empting of space and personnel forced us to look to other resources for expansion. Simultaneously, the faculty field instructors with sharply focused educational goals were ready to move toward a curriculum that would envision the social worker of the future and the challenge of preparation for the job demands.[6]

It became clear that the traditional agency, offering a specialized service, could no longer prepare students for the demands of social work as currently evolving. As understood and implemented in this school, the training center provides: (1) an enriched learning environment with a corps of teachers; (2) a range of agencies from which selected, appropriate learning opportunities can be drawn (in contrast to the traditional one-agency environment); (3) the possibility for students to relate themselves closely to a total neighborhood environment where they can sense the dimensions of the problems encountered by families as well as the impinging forces that generate and cultivate these problems; and (4) a vantage point for defining social problems, identifying differentially the interventive strategy appropriate to problem amelioration, and for teaching students beginning practice skills in these social work technologies.

The school is now inclined to understand the first year of field teach-

[5] Walter L. Kindelsperger and Helen Cassidy, *Social Work Training Centers: Tentative Analysis of the Structure and Learning Environment* (New Orleans: Tulane University School of Social Work, September, 1966).

[6] Walter L. Kindelsperger, "Responsible Entry into the Profession—Some Current Issues," *Journal of Education for Social Work*, Vol. 2, No. 1 (Spring, 1966), pp. 43-45.

ing and learning as a continuum that begins with a heavy emphasis on the knowledge, values, and intellectual grasp of the profession—its development and responsibility in society—and on its methodology and the organization of social work and social welfare services. The focus changes gradually during the year into a clinical application of the content.

Students are introduced to a general conception of the welfare function in society today by a variety of observations, participant observations, and study of particular social problems of the community, neighborhood, and families. Student reports and seminar discussions are used to promote, clarify, and insure learning relevant to the stated objectives. This background provides the basis for differentiating and defining functions assigned to social work, for specifying detail of these functions, and for indicating the rationale for knowledge content in social work activities. Students are introduced systematically to the basic problems as they appear in the life activities and situations of human beings whose well-being is the basic concern of the profession.

The prototype neighborhood-based training center suggests a central agency serving as the "hub," and a constellation of other agencies and services drawn into the total operation. A fully developed center will likely have between 45 and 50 students and some five or six faculty members. All first-year students at Tulane are placed in neighborhood-based training centers that are focused around a range of services offered to the neighborhood population.

Gradual assumption of and follow-through on professional responsibility in the methods or technologies of social work calls for experiences with an individual or family and with a small group. In addition, students gain awareness of the community and how the milieu enhances or impedes individual and group goals. The field instructor assigned to the student group maintains overall responsibility for teaching the students and for coordination, with special consultants assigned to supply enrichment to student learning. The latter faculty members include the group work teacher, who serves as consultant in that methodology, and the research consultant for the student research project in the field setting.

Research is introduced in the first semester to emphasize its tie-in with practice. This timing exploits the student's natural curiosity about the environment, the people, and the problems he sees around him. The research experience provides him with a scientific approach in seeking answers to professional problems.

The setting is a rich one for learning. A wide range of social services are available. There is a sizeable number of students and faculty. The faculty must be full-time social work educators to assume the teaching role demanded. The faculty have a variety of areas of expertness that can be shared by all. The student group represents various learning patterns, special interests, and flairs. The setting is equally geared to afford a common body of experiences and to individualize students according to their learning level and métier.

Obviously, such an operation requires coordination. A senior faculty member assigned to the training center serves as the school's representative and as coordinator of education. Her responsibilities include insuring that the curriculum objectives for student learning are met, organizing and coordinating learning experiences, providing direction to other faculty in planning, and serving as liaison with the central agency, or hub, as well as with the other services that make up the complex.

CURRENT EXPECTATIONS OF THE ROLE OF COORDINATOR OF FIELD INSTRUCTION

Summary—Rationale of the Tulane Plan

The experiment at Tulane over the last several years has attempted to test the meaning of full-time faculty appointments for all learning experiences, whether the mode of learning is classroom or field. The field instruction faculty was brought in on this basis for many reasons, not least the fact that field instruction is a sequence in its own right with a body of material to be taught.

Field instructors enjoy full-fledged faculty status, are appointed at all levels of academic rank depending on age, experience, and education. They may work for tenure standing. They participate in all basic faculty decisions, take their places on important faculty committees. When they make meaningful contributions to such sequences as Normal Development, the Methods of Social Work, and Research, it is on the basis of their knowledge and their needs as teachers. They move in and out of classroom teaching.

The goal for educational preparation of field instructors is a full year of preparation beyond the master's degree. In the future, they will be expected to have the doctoral degree in addition to clinical experience and interests. During this transitional period, the school is attempting to bridge the gap by building in an advanced year in clinical teaching. This plan is now in the early stages of implementation. The same expectations for scholarship exist for field instructors in relation to their area of practice. Several field instructors regularly produce papers.

What we are doing amounts to an experiment that will demonstrate the result of having full-time faculty at all levels and in all modes of teaching. We propose to find out what will happen if all field instructors with the level of education described hold full-time faculty appointments.

Within this total context, then, we now see the role of the coordinator of field instruction at Tulane in a very different way than it was seen several years ago. The following material will attempt to describe the current activities.

Educational dimensions

The requirement for educational coordination is foremost. The coordinator of field instruction works with a body of educators committed to teaching the field mode of the curriculum. Responsibilities are not unlike those of other sequence leadership roles except for the dimensions and the number of faculty involved.

Weekly meetings with field instructors are set up in order to engage them in the course-charting for the field curriculum—planning the sequence, implementing educational objectives, devising learning experiences to reach designated objectives, making decisions about pedagogical devices appropriate to the plans. The continuing work of timing experiences, testing their validity, identifying core concepts to be taught differentially via the experiences available in the different centers, and measuring student progress is omnipresent.

Coordination of work and clarification of goals with other faculty members, who play a direct consultative role in the field setting or who teach in a specific sequence, is frequently carried out through cross-curriculum committees. These committees are made up of class and field faculty and are organized around content and objectives. The goal is curriculum implementation and development. The coordinator is active on these committees but also maintains an overview of factors not routinely found on committee agendas in order to keep attuned to overall goals and avoid the danger of snags.

A final aspect of the educational role is a special kind of work, largely administrative, that is carried on, both individually and in a group, with those faculty members who are assigned the permanent task of training center coordination.

Administration and planning

The development of a corps of faculty-based field instructors and the acceptance of the training center as the environment for field learning has resulted in a new type of relationship of the school to the agencies. More planning occurs at the policy-making level. State and regional offices of official agencies are deeply involved. Since our interests lie in more comprehensive plans, we are seeking authorization and innovation in introducing new programs, finding new ways in which our training centers can collaborate, designing centers that cut across departmental lines but involve several departments in their operation.

We are more involved with personnel of offices at the state and regional levels (e.g., of the Department of Health, Education, and Welfare) with follow-through with corollary personnel at the state and local levels. An obvious readiness to collaborate on the part of high- and middle-level management is most rewarding. Agencies welcome innovating ideas from the school provided these have been tested and are

154

supported by substantiating evidence of their practical value.[7] Agency-school relations have become collegial in nature. Student education serves as the focal point, but the mutual sharing in posing the right questions and searching for answers is salutary and indicative of a profession uniting around vital challenges.

The maintenance function

While I have highlighted some of the newer trends and emphases of the task of the coordinator of field instruction, this does not indicate a lessening in the continuing job with local agencies. It is primarily a difference in emphasis and kind of collaboration. There are still problems about space, especially with larger numbers of students. There is still the need to have agency cooperation and sanction for students to use their facilities, especially for drawing on their client group for giving service. These problems somehow seem more amenable to negotiation when the atmosphere is not charged with an urgent need for their personnel to assume the direct teaching jobs.

Aside from these practical issues, there is an ongoing function of the school, as represented in the role of coordinator of field instruction, which goes under the sometimes dubious title of "public relations." The term is used here in its best sense: keeping the public informed and assuring that channels of communication are open for a two-way flow of information. A community is responsive to a school and its progress, provided the community is made partner to both. The following activities may be useful here: a coordinating committee made up of key people from the social work community to serve as liaison between school and community; a large, school-sponsored gathering once or twice annually that brings together agency executives collaborating with the school for a joint social-educational experience (e.g., reports may be given by the school on recent or prospective activities to keep the practice domain abreast of educational developments); and invitations issued by the school to agencies when a lecturer of note comes to the community under school sponsorship.

Too much cannot be said in favor of an open and free communication between school and community. Regardless of its prowess or educational standing, a school cannot progress in a healthy manner unless the social work community supports it. The coordinator of field instruction must assume responsibility for doing this work in the name of the school as a key part of her function.

---

[7] Perhaps the era is of the essence in effecting this collaboration. Seldom has a profession been so faced with crises. We are haunted by manpower shortages, harassed by internal and external pressures to find answers to the big questions: How much preparation for which jobs? What is the relationship of education (and what type) to functional job expectations? If disaster or the threat of it unites men, we are at the very apex of opportunity for fruitful collaboration.

155

THE DIRECTOR OF FIELD WORK—ADMINISTRATOR AND EDUCATOR

RUTH WERNER

THOSE OF US who are engaged in social work education recognize that there are as many dissimilarities as similarities in the structuring of schools of social work. The following is the description of the Department of Field Work at one school. At the School of Applied Social Sciences, Case Western Reserve University, the Department of Field Work is relatively new. It came into being July 1, 1965, and is staffed by a director and a secretary.

The Case Western Reserve University School of Applied Social Sciences had 200 students in the master's program in the fall of 1967 and 199 in field placement (121 in casework placements, 38 in community organization placements, and 40 in group work placements). The school works with 43 cooperating agencies, utilizing 66 agency field instructors and 17 field instructors employed by the school (hereafter referred to as faculty field instructors).

Although the Department of Field Work is new, the school celebrated its 50th anniversary in 1966, and field instruction has been an integral part of the education of social work students since the school's beginning. Responsibility for work with agencies was previously carried by the faculty in the casework, group work, and community organization areas. Of course, there had always been some coordination of work with community agencies, most recently through the office of the dean: letters were sent out to determine how many students agencies could accept and some contacts were made with agency representatives.

RUTH WERNER is director of the department of Field Work at Case Western Reserve University School of Applied Social Sciences. This paper was originally presented at the Council on Social Work Education Sixteenth Annual Program Meeting in Minneapolis, Minnesota, January, 1968.

I mention history because, in setting up a new department, it is important to build on that which is sound and has stood the school in good stead over the years. Thus, in structuring the new Department of Field Work, stress was placed on the department's cooperation with the practice areas. Certain responsibilities for the program of field instruction are shared by the director of the Field Work Department and the chairmen of the three practice areas. These include the following:

1. Decision-making regarding the acceptance of an agency. The appraisal of the level of practice within the agency rests with the casework, group work, or community organization area.

2. Placement planning. This may be delegated to the areas, from which the director of Field Work then receives reports. (The director of Field Work, as a member of the casework area, takes direct responsibility for placements and many other facets of work in this area.)

3. Educational opportunities for field instructors. Each area sets up meetings for the consideration of issues specific to that practice area; the director of Field Work may serve as a facilitator for such meetings.

   The director of Field Work is responsible for those planned programs which cut across practice areas, such as meetings for new field instructors and general meetings for cooperating agencies and field instructors.

4. Development of a curriculum of field instruction. The development of content related to practice, including techniques and the conceptual framework for teaching in the field, is the responsibility of the areas. The director of Field Work is responsible for seeing that a curriculum is developed by each practice area.

5. Liaison with cooperating agencies. The assignment of faculty to carry the liaison responsibility with cooperating agencies originates with the practice areas. The responsibility is generally carried by classroom faculty, thus affording a link to practice. If more than one area is working with a given cooperating agency, the director of Field Work will assign one faculty person to handle the liaison with agency administration or with a person designated by the agency. Both area chairmen and the director of Field Work are, of course, available for consultation with the faculty liaison people.

6. Employment of faculty field instructors. Again, the chairmen of the various areas are the ones to assess the level of practice of prospective candidates. Likewise, area chairmen share with the director of Field Work the responsibility for ongoing appraisal of the functioning of faculty field instructors including, when indicated, recommendations for termination of employment or for promotion.

Those are the shared responsibilities. Certain administrative responsibilities are clearly delegated to the director of Field Work. These include:

1. Developing a set of policies for work with cooperating agencies.
2. Developing working materials such as a handbook for cooperating agencies.
3. Maintaining records on cooperating agencies and agency field instructors.
4. Carrying administrative responsibility for faculty field instructors. For example, clearance on outside assignments that faculty field instructors may wish to assume and end-of-the-year conferences, which may serve in lieu of a conference with the dean, with each faculty field instructor.
5. Keeping the dean informed on the work of the Department of Field Work. Involving him appropriately in decision-making (i.e., whether to terminate field placement and withdraw from a co-operating agency)

One of the strains in the position of director of Field Work is the feeling that colleagues look upon the position primarily as that of a problem-solver. For example, when a relationship with an agency must be severed, the problem is turned over to the director; when it is going relatively smoothly, the director may have minimal involvement. The educational functions do rest to a large extent with the practice areas; however, a Department of Field Work exists not only for administrative purposes, but to enhance the learning opportunities for students in the field. Therefore, a primary responsibility of a director of Field Work lies in the area of professional education.

In order to assist the director of Field Work in fulfilling her responsibilities as an educator, our dean appointed an Advisory Committee to the Field Work Department. This committee was made up of a representative from each of the practice areas and two faculty field instructors nominated by the director of the Department of Field Work. This committee has given attention to: development of criteria for agencies in which faculty field instructors are placed; revision of criteria for field agencies and agency field instructors; the nature and content of educational opportunities that should be provided for field instructors; and revision of the description of the Department of Field Work.

Three areas in which the director of Field Work at Case Western Reserve University functions as an educator are:

1. Providing educational opportunities for field instructors.
2. Working with faculty field instructors to clarify their role as educators.
3. Stimulating, facilitating, and evaluating experimentation in field instruction.

The importance of the field instructor in the education of students is evidenced by evaluative comments made by students graduating over the past three years in response to questionnaires tapping their reaction to the master's curriculum at the School of Applied Social Sciences. A high proportion of students reported finding field instruction one of the most valuable educational experiences they had. This confirms Charlotte Towle's statement that "the nature of this relationship is decisively important for the student's initial orientation to and continued use of the school as a whole."[1] So the work of the director of Field Work with field instructors assumes particular importance.

As stated above, the practice areas share in providing educational opportunities for field instructors; however, meetings for new field instructors are under the leadership of the director of Field Work. It has always been our practice to provide some orientation for new field instructors, specifically an overview of the curriculum and an understanding of the evaluation process. In the last several years the meetings for new field instructors have been expanded. A short, relevant bibliography is provided along with specific assignments for each of several sessions that deal with the following subjects:

1. Orientation to the role of social work educator;
2. The concept of educational diagnosis;
3. The selection of learning experiences for social work students;
4. Responses to learning experiences in the field; and
5. Evaluation as an educational process.

This orientation series has been modified on the basis of: experience, responses to a questionnaire distributed to participants, and increased freedom for the field instructors to initiate discussion of their own concerns. An example was a discussion that revolved around whether individualizing the learner smacks of therapy. One new field instructor commented, "We don't psychologize our students in community organization." This provided an opportunity for clarifying the differences between individualizing the learner and treating the learner. Another illustration occurred in relation to a presentation of the learning experiences provided in a hospital setting. One new field instructor saw the demands as so overwhelming that he felt only a second-year student could cope with this stressful setting. Another new field instructor reported that first-year students were functioning successfully in an equally stressful hospital setting. Out of such exchanges comes awareness of common and/or unique problems in coping with learners.

The director also plans general meetings for all field instructors and representatives of the cooperating agencies who carry responsibility for liaison between agency and school. Curriculum issues must be explored if field instructors are to help students integrate theory into practice. In the fall of 1966, we provided field instructors with a broad overview of the curriculum design and an opportunity to discuss implications for field teaching. Instructors responded to the challenge, but

---

[1] Charlotte Towle, *The Learner in Education for the Professions* (Chicago: University of Chicago Press, 1954), p. 139.

not without some concern about moving into new content areas and adopting new methods. In responding to a questionnaire in June, 1967, they unanimously requested more information regarding course content. So in the fall of 1967 a series of three meetings was set up in order to provide an opportunity for all interested field instructors to get acquainted with the content of the required course sequences.

Following the Annual Program Meeting of the Council on Social Work Education in 1967, the director of the Field Work Department planned a session in which major themes were reported but emphasis was given to field instruction. The success of this presentation prompted the suggestion that it be repeated annually. Study groups provide another means of involving all field instructors in order to enhance their knowledge and skill. One such study group met over a two-year period to discuss the use of group meetings in field instruction. A professor who has responsibility for teaching content on small group theory in the master's program served as resource person for this study group. Another of these study groups developed a set of criteria for measuring performance of second-year casework students that has been adopted for use by the casework area.

The second major area in which the director of Field Work functions as an educator is in her work with the faculty field instructors. Faculty field instructors are usually not new to field instruction, but for many the experience is the instructor's first in becoming part of an educational system, i.e., in a school of social work in a university. There are many differences from employment in a social agency with its hierarchical structure. In a school of social work there is fluidity within the structure, and colleague relationships replace the hierarchical relationships that the instructor has known. Faculty field instructors need help in becoming accustomed to functioning within a new system; sometimes they yearn for past structured relationships and at other times they react against the semblance of structure in the new setting. Becoming part of this new system is complicated because the field instructor is still also working within an agency. In our particular school, most of the agencies in which we have faculty field instructors have problems which mitigate against using agency field instructors. Therefore, it is incumbent upon the director of Field Work to help the new field instructor handle the frustrations inherent in these settings so that a good learning opportunity can be provided for students.

This problem of being a part of two systems also creates conflicts over role identification. We recognize that the agency-employed field instructor has a primary identification with the agency and a secondary identification with the role of instructor. The faculty field instructor must have sufficient identification with the agency to promote a range of learning opportunities for the student, yet, by virtue of the fact that he is employed by the school, he must also have a solid identification with the educational system. His responsibility for the education of social work students goes beyond field practice. He must be capable of assessing the student's overall functioning. There was a time at our school when faculty field instructors had the unenviable position of carrying no more responsibility for the educational function than did the agency field instructors, yet they had more students. This also often created conflict for the student, who knew that the field instructor was employed by the school and yet the student could not look to him for help except as it related to field practice. However, with the assumption of greater responsibility comes conflict of a different sort for the field instructor. Is he too powerful? Again, the director of Field Work can help the field instructor develop his capacity to use his responsibility productively. Consultations may cover the learning patterns of individual students; a student may be referred to the director of Field Work if it seems that the working relationship between student and field instructor could be facilitated by contact with a third person. Thus, the instructor is relieved of some of the stress that grows out of feeling that he is perhaps too powerful in relation to the future of a particular student.

Implicit in the above is conflict over status. The faculty field instructor is often perceived and/or perceives himself as "low man on the totem pole." We have made some attempts to cope with this problem, while recognizing that we have not solved it. Through regularly scheduled meetings in which faculty field instructors can discuss their concerns and their goals, they gain a sense of group identity which they indicate has enhanced their sense of well-being. Of course, this is not enough, and in 1966 we took the step of defining criteria for promotion for faculty field instructors, using the major headings adapted by full professors as a basis for moving up the academic ladder. These criteria are: fulfillment of the role of a faculty member; teaching competence; mastery of field; contribution to the development of new knowledge; and contribution to professional and community service.

Another means of enhancing the self-image of the faculty field instructor is through making use of his expertise. In the orientation sessions referred to above, faculty field instructors participate, presenting from their own experience examples of the nature of learning experiences and their rationale and of the nature of the student's response and ways of helping the student to cope most effectively. Faculty field instructor expertise is also put to use through assignments to working committees throughout the school.

A third major area in which the director of Field Work functions as an educator is the area of experimentation. At Case Western Reserve University we maintain, for the most part, traditional field instruction in the three practice areas—casework, group work, and community organization—however, we are encouraging experimentation that will enhance the students' learning. This experimentation often takes place within the field units, but not exclusively there. The role of director of

Field Work is to stimulate, facilitate, and encourage evaluation of experimentation.

For example, we have a specialist on our faculty who has the responsibility for enhancing our knowledge of the problems of the aged and services to meet their needs. Three voluntary agencies which serve the aged provide field instruction in casework and group work, and none has more than three students. Under the stimulation of the specialist on aging, these agencies were brought together to plan joint sessions for their students, on common problems and on a range of services to meet the needs of the aging. These students as well as other interested students working with the aged may attend. The agencies are enthusiastic; we at the school see these meetings as a means of broadening the learning opportunities for the students.

Although our students have a primary assignment in one practice area, we are encouraging exposure to more than one practice method. A number of agencies provide field instruction to students in at least two methods and we have used various means to broaden learning opportunities. When we have in one agency faculty field instructors in more than one method, we plan for student practice experience in a second method. For example, a student in a casework unit at the Juvenile Court expressed interest in working with a group in the Detention Home, and we arranged for her to have consultation with a faculty field instructor in group work on her work with this group. In another case, a student in community organization, through consultation with a faculty field instructor in group work in the settlement where the student was placed, was provided with experience in the use of the group as a means of helping individuals in social functioning.

We talk about our desire to achieve integration of learning in all areas of the curriculum. A faculty field instructor, identified with the school and its curriculum, can often do more innovating in this area than an agency instructor. An example is the placement of second-year casework students in the emergency room of a hospital for observation of stress points for patients and for intervention when appropriate. The students' observations, transmitted to the administrator by prior arrangement, will be the basis for policy formulation to improve patient care in the emergency room. Thus, the students have a first-hand experience as change agents.

Our students who return to the public field after educational leaves are often asked to assume responsibility for supervision and staff development within a year of graduation. We are aware that we have not prepared them to meet these demands. We are now beginning with second-year casework students, who have had work experience prior to entering professional education, to provide them with an opportunity simultaneously to enhance their practice skills in casework and to carry beginning responsibility for the supervision of an untrained, inexperienced staff member. The use of the group in teaching this unit of students provides an opportunity to observe the learning patterns of four untrained, inexperienced staff members. This, coupled with course content in Supervision and Staff Development, will, it is hoped, provide the base for further professional growth and readiness to assume a different level of responsibility in the field.

Perhaps our most important experimental program is our Training Center, located in an inner-city community, in which we have 22 students in the three practice methods. We have great hopes that the faculty field instructors, under the direction of the associate dean, will enrich our knowledge of how we can most effectively provide social work students with learning opportunities across method lines.

In conclusion, important and demanding as the administrative responsibilities of a director of Field Work may be, the primary responsibility is to enhance the educational opportunities for students in field practice. In order to do this, the director must provide stimulation for the field instructors, who, in turn, are working directly with the students. This involves providing agency-employed field instructors with basic knowledge of curriculum and learning theory. It involves helping school-employed field instructors to fulfill their role as educators. It involves creating a climate in which experimentation can take place. This, then, is an overview of the work of one Department of Field Work.

HELPING FIELD INSTRUCTORS RETOOL WHEN A SCHOOL CHANGES ITS APPROACH TO THE TEACHING OF METHODS

JOSEPHINE DiPAOLA

THIS IS THE fourth year of teaching in our revised curriculum in which it has been our goal to prepare the generalist for social work practice, and helping field teachers retool has now progressed beyond the initial phase of implementing a new curriculum design. In that first important step we moved from the drawing board to the field of action. To the extent that we could, we had spelled out the theory which was to guide our actions and projected a practicum that brought together our experience with the practice methods then known. It represented an innovative and experimental thrust, and it required a new set of tools to implement it.

As I look back over three-and-a-half years, I realize that this was only the beginning. Retooling has been a continuing process, and we are still engaged in it. We are still working to secure a better fit of theory and practice and to bring about a more successful fusion of the two. At the same time, other themes, sub-themes, and drives have come into prominence. These have made an impression, and have continued to modify our curriculum while the generalist concept of practice has become a central and stable focal cornerstone. The instruments which we have employed to give shape to our changes have had to be flexible and varied to permit nuances of theme and form, and at the same time to maintain a semblance of balance and unity in our curriculum.

Before presenting our retooling process, I think it is important to identify some forces and influences which are pushing our profession and schools to examine and modify our practice approaches.

JOSEPHINE DiPAOLA is director of field instruction at the School of Social Work of the University of Southern California. This paper was originally presented at the Council on Social Work Education Seventeenth Annual Program Meeting in Cleveland, Ohio, January, 1969.

1. The pressing issues and problems of our society have created new imperatives for delivering social services which meet the needs of vital sub-groups of our society. Turner has suggested a re-orientation which emphasizes the concept of social rehabilitation, in which the social worker would participate actively in human development in an attempt to reach ghetto residents unable to benefit from established institutional services.[1] In fact, field instruction units are being established in new service centers where innovative approaches are being devised to meet current needs. Frequently, however, these centers lack a defined structure for giving the services and a model for articulating the role of the social work practitioner. Furthermore, students are being placed in such centers immediately after the initiation of such services. Field teachers frequently have had little or no prior practice experience in such operations, although they are usually experienced in field teaching.

2. The knowledge explosion has continued to excite and to frustrate us. All teachers, including field teachers, must not only continue to seek out new knowledge, but must pursue its potential application to social work theory and practice. The cycle of acquiring knowledge, working it over, and assimilating it into our professional behavior is generally not done in isolation. Rather, it is accomplished in interaction with professional peers in school and agency. While the field instructor devotes proportionately less time to theory building and its validation than the classroom teacher, he still requires a broad exposure to what has filtered through in the form of new knowledge. This new knowledge has to be made explicit to practice and the teaching of practice. To be effective, it must be incorporated into the delivery of services of the agency in which the practice takes place. The field instructor must be engaged on all these levels.

3. Assuming that our basic aim is the preparation of the student to cope with a changing world, we need to continue to devise frames of references which will encourage him to: (1) think in a disciplined way about what he knows or does not know, and the applicability of his knowledge; (2) identify and factor out the components of the problem-solving processes in which he is involved; and (3) build conceptual guides for thinking and doing, which derive from a sense of security and mastery of the professional role. With the field teacher lies the responsibility for having the scientific base from which to teach this, and the imagination and skill to teach productively.

4. Today, students are active participants in formulating their learn-

---

[1] John B. Turner, "In Response to Change: Social Work at the Crossroads," *Social Work,* Volume 13, Number 3 (July, 1968), pp. 7-9.

ing goals and in influencing the direction and content of curricula. Their expectations for change generally go beyond ours. We think that we are moving too rapidly to validate what we have. They think we are moving too slowly, with too little focus on their immediate concerns. It should be noted that students have had no questions whatsoever about the "rightness" of our movement toward generalist practice. Rather, they have been a force in expecting field instructors to implement the whole continuum of modalities of practice in every course of field instruction. If teachers do not take the initiative for reviewing the criteria for selecting one modality in comparison with another, students make explicit the concepts they have been learning about this and request that they have the opportunity to test these in their practice course. Moreover, students in different placements compare notes on their respective experiences and make known their own demands for experience.

All these forces have pressed for expression and action concurrent with our retooling for the generalist practice highlighted in our revised curriculum. They have tended to challenge and rechallenge us as we continued to study whether we were indeed on the right track, or whether we were following a road that led nowhere. These forces have also stimulated us to devise varied and flexible models for teaching the new curriculum.

THE RETOOLING TASK

We come now to a consideration of the nature and size of the retooling task of field instructors. What learning and teaching behaviors were required of them? What parts of the task were immediate, and what parts might be viewed as being accomplished over a period of time? How does a school help teachers accomplish these tasks effectively?

A list of the demands made of field teachers by the new curriculum will provide a picture of the scope of the change and of some of the components of the task.

1. The new frame of reference, with its related knowledge and theories, had to be acquired by all field teachers and key persons in settings in which field courses were taught.

2. Beyond the acquisition of knowledge and theory, teachers needed opportunities to apply their learning to practice in order to achieve some mastery in new modalities of practice.

3. Field teachers have had to be change agents in the settings in which they practiced and taught, so that new modalities of practice—which agencies found to be valid—might become an integral part of the delivery of services. The school has had to support

167

this change by working directly with administrators and other key personnel.

4. Assuming that an expanded competence in using new practice approaches could be acquired by field instructors, and also assuming that agency structures could be modified to encompass them, the field teacher was required to develop new field courses in which some old and some new aspects might be combined and taught. Experiences would have to be selected, content would have to be spelled out and organized, and the basic concepts to be taught would have to be factored out.

5. The change in curriculum required our field teachers to become more sophisticated about practice research and to participate in the evaluation of the new curriculum.

6. Field teachers were under pressure from various sources. Classroom teachers pressed for the teaching of the same concepts taught in the classroom. Students wanted the opportunity to practice in all the modalities, as well as have class and field learning be concurrent. Field teachers had their own pressures to evolve field courses which possessed internal consistency, logic, and flow, and which would be conducive to learning.

In listing some of the demands that the new curriculum made on field instructors, one inevitably reaches the point where one must ask whether it is possible and probable to recruit field teachers in sufficient numbers to meet such demands. We are asking for field instructors who have aptitude for scholarship, possess security in the practice of a broad range of interventive methods, are able to identify and teach principles and concepts from specific practice tasks, and are able to evaluate and influence the delivery of social services in social agencies. The conclusion one reaches is that these demands are formidable in terms of the nature and size of the tasks and are not always met.

RETOOLING STAGES

In our school we have 49 field instructors, 15 of whom are full-time teachers. Approximately one-half of our students are taught by full-time teachers. Since about two-thirds of our field instructors are part-time teachers and in the employ of agencies, considerable effort is devoted to educational role and content. Retooling for the revised curriculum has continued to reinforce new perspectives toward practice, and new concepts for teaching it. I bring out this point because our curriculum change derived historically from two movements: (1) the thrust from social agencies and social work practitioners to employ a range of interventive modalities to meet differential needs, conditions, and purposes; and (2) the efforts of social work practice theoreticians and teachers to bring to this subject the knowledge insights from many fields, and to engage in beginning levels of conceptualizing a generic practice in order to provide some guides and models for action. To be sure, both of these developments have been uneven and have not meshed completely, yet the two movements have become interdependent for the transformation of the practice and the symbolic representation of that practice in theory building to meet the needs of a changing world and its changing institutions. Teachers are, in a sense, the mediators of these interdependent processes because they must engage in thinking about practice if it is to be taught, and what they teach must be confirmed through practice.

Looking back over three-and-one-half years of the process of retooling, successive stages may be identified, which I would like to present in terms of Whitehead's conceptualization.[2]

1. The stage of "romance," which generates new perceptions and conceptions. The new conceptual model provides a base for stimulating new thought and understanding of a subject area. New images and prototypes move into the center of consideration.

2. The stage of "precision," which pinpoints the directions, problems, and issues, and which requires more intensive analysis and "exactness of formulation." Bit by bit, through study, application, disciplined examination, and evaluation, there evolves a system for organizing and articulating relevant principles and concepts.

3. The stage of "generalization," often referred to as the stage of synthesis or integration, which reflects the incorporation of the change into a set of behaviors.

I would like to describe some characteristic approaches to retooling in each of these stages.

The stage of romance

Originally, the formulation of the generalist approach of our revised curriculum was articulated for all teachers, executives, students, and others. Immediate and longer-range goals were set up for implementing the curriculum in successive steps. In field instruction, we sought to provide for each student experience with two out of three modalities of social work practice, namely, work with individuals, family groups, and non-related peer groups. Second-year placements sought to extend and deepen learning in the two modalities experienced in the first year and add the opportunity to learn the third modality of practice. The second step in the progression was to expect that all three modalities be incorporated in every field instruction course, with the expectation that there might be more emphasis in one modality as compared with another. The third step was to spell out and provide experience in community work which, by and large, was already a component in the teaching of most field courses.

---

[2] Alfred North Whitehead, *The Aims of Education* (New York: A Mentor Book, 1956), pp. 29-30.

169

In the beginning, then, the emphasis was to think of practice methods in an interrelated way and to try out less familiar modalities. We held formal seminars to impart to field instructors the new curriculum prospectus, the nature of the change envisioned, and the content projected for new field courses. The major assignment of these seminars was for each field instructor to take on a practice project in order to learn a new modality of practice. They presented their projects and learning to one another. Since all had expertise in one or two modalities and were learners in others, they learned from and taught one another. Classroom teachers also brought their insights to the revised curriculum. As casework and group work field instructors reviewed and factored out their own and others' practice values, purposes, goals, and action patterns, they hammered out significant similarities and differences in the methods. Knowledge input helped to underpin and illuminate the new frame of reference.

Field teachers also contributed directly to classroom teaching, where case materials from field courses were introduced in specific sessions with classroom and field teachers collaborating in the teaching. Field teachers became members of the Practice Teachers' Sequence Committee in the continuing development of this sequence. Through their liaison function with agencies, classroom teachers also intimately followed developments in the field. A conscious effort was made throughout to articulate principles and concepts taught in both field and class and to highlight criteria for selection of one modality or another. In essence, this was still the "trying out" phase to "see what would happen."

This was also the stage in which impetus for generalist practice was generated by our students. Students tend to be ready and eager for innovations. They did not have the doubts that some experienced practitioners tended to have about whether the new formulation would indeed stand up, whether the quality of practice was being eroded, whether a broadened content could be encompassed in the MSW program, whether these emerging social workers would be equipped to enter the profession adequately prepared, etc. With characteristic energy and high expectations, the students threw themselves into these new learning opportunities and came to feel deprived if they did not have an assignment in a particular method. They seized upon the challenge for defending one approach in comparison with another. In many ways, they pushed all of us into moving faster to achieve our goal for providing opportunities to practice in the entire continuum of methods.

Concurrently, there was a marked expansion of teaching methods. The new thrust lent itself to more extensive use of observational experiences, to create models to be used as prototypes for units of learning, to expand and enrich methods of group teaching where tutorial teaching had been the predominant method, to utilize more consultants in direct teaching, etc. Many field teachers worked together and involved their respective field centers in complementing and supplementing experience for more students. There resulted many imaginative innovations in teaching methodology, which made each field course individual and exciting.

The stage of precision

Retooling efforts of the first stage resulted in a proliferation of content in field courses. In some instances, the field course retained its basic format and there was added the opportunity to observe or to have a limited experience in a modality not previously included. In other instances, the core assignment was reevaluated and expanded to make possible more options to utilize a number of modalities of intervention instead of a standard method. In still other instances, there was a complete departure from established orientations, and a new beginning was made to lay the groundwork for considering the possible use of all modalities.

In this first stage, field teachers tended to try out the additive approach rather than reorganize field courses in their entirety. As they moved forward and examined closely what they had, they became more interested in designing new courses rather than extending the old. This was not characteristic of all field instructors, yet it was characteristic of our best teachers. The latter experienced a sense of excitement in dealing with the potential for multi-dimensional practice on an abstract level as well as on an operational level. They joined forces with classroom teachers and other field teachers who were also interested in pursuing the subject further. Even while their own learning continued at an accelerated pace, they tended to become freer in trying out new ideas in field instruction courses. As a result, a vast amount of specific content found its way into field courses. This led to some confusion and much frustration because all the content could not be encompassed and organized immediately.

The second stage, then, identified by Whitehead as the stage of precision, called for continuing and intensive work by teachers as a group to analyze their new experiences, the factoring out of concepts which illuminated new practice approaches, and the suggesting of guides for organizing the content for learning-teaching purposes. The field teachers worked with each other in small groups and with teachers in other sequences, particularly in the classroom practice sequence, where a revision of syllabus was undertaken.

This engagement led to specific outcomes. As our experience with trying out the new orientation grew, field teachers were faced with the task of examining more systematically what they were teaching, when, and in what sequence. They had to begin to put this down in two forms: (1) on an operational basis in the form of a revision of the *Manual of Field Instruction* of the School; and (2) in a syllabus which would project content to be included in all courses of field instruction.

The revision of our *Manual of Field Instruction* was not undertaken immediately after the adoption of the revised curriculum. We wanted to try out the new aspects of the curriculum before we did this. When we became committed to the direction we were taking, we began to think of setting down our current objectives for field instruction and the standards and expectations for performance of students at different points in the MSW program. We also had to evolve an instrument for evaluating the performance of students. Small committees of interested field instructors began working on these formulations. Their work, in turn, provided subjects for institutes and workshops for the entire field. This work is still in process.

While the development of new and revised syllabi has been characteristic of all sequences, the development of a syllabus in the field instruction sequence has presented a particular challenge because we have had to engage a large number of teachers in different parts of the task, and they have been at different stages of development as field teachers. Groups have had to get together to compare experiences and, eventually, to achieve congruence in working toward the same course objectives and to define tasks to be undertaken and assigned with reference to working on a syllabus. A concurrent demand has been that all field units in our program must achieve our first major goal—the teaching of the entire range of practice modalities in field courses. We can say confidently that we have achieved this goal by the end of the third year.

Another dimension of this stage of retooling is related to our research efforts on evaluation. Field teachers have been engaged in two aspects of evaluation. On a broad and comprehensive basis, we have been developing an evaluation instrument that attempts to measure the content that was taught in each sequence, the degree of emphasis in each area of content, and the ratings of students in relation to content, emphasis, and what, in retrospect, should have been the emphasis. In this research task, a committee of field instructors has had to devise for the schedule content items that reflected the objectives of the field instruction sequence in the revised curriculum. A research consultant worked with the committee. Field teachers not only participated in setting up the research instruments but have been respondents in the research process.

In addition to this effort, the field instruction sequence has been responsible for evolving an instrument for evaluating student performance that was based on the expectations for performance at the end of each semester of the MSW program. A research specialist has been a member of the committee which spearheaded this activity.

Students have undertaken research projects in selected areas of inquiry into our curriculum. One group of students studied our advisory system as perceived by students and advisors. Another cluster of students examined the students' appraisal, following receipt of the MSW degree, of specific and integrated aspects of the practice methods. A doctoral dissertation is presently being carried out for testing ten concepts learned by the graduates of two classes in the revised curriculum to determine what has been their experience with these concepts in practice since graduation. Five MSW students are developing a small research design which will gear into this dissertation. These research efforts on the part of students reflect their interest in assessing experience with the revised curriculum; also, their questions have stimulated us to more careful inquiry and their findings have influenced some changes.

The second stage of precision is by far the most extensive and time-consuming stage of retooling. We are still engaged in it after three and one-half years. Though we are well into many facets for forging more precise tools, many projects have not been completed. Occasionally, we revert to the first stage and ask a question which takes us back to the beginning. In other ways, we are well into the third stage of implementation.

The stage of generalization

The third and final stage of retooling is directed toward generalization or integration of the change. At this point, we can identify numerous teaching-learning behaviors which have already undergone change in the direction sought and other behaviors which are in the process of becoming integrated at a higher level of behaving. Let me make these points explicit by some examples.

First, in our school today there is little pointed reference on the part of students, faculty, and agency personnel to the validity of teaching a continuum of practice methods instead of specializations. That the practitioner needs to employ differential approaches to problem-solving, and that the student needs to be prepared for a generalist practice which permits flexibility of approach and development of sensitivity to changing needs and situations, have been accepted generally. In actuality, we are preparing students to enter current practice, not future practice. At the same time, the concept of the generalist is not of one social work practitioner being a replica of every other. The extension and elaboration of a continuum of modalities of practice has led to a higher level of generalization and conceptualization in all social work practice and the knowledge and skill to select one or several constructs provided for more effective deployment of a particular methodology. Specialization is still possible and may be built on this base.

We have been able to incorporate this frame of reference into different agency settings (traditional and new) and to fields of service including prevention, human development, crisis intervention, etc. In a newly established service center which serves minority groups in the poverty sub-culture, reaching out to clientele is accomplished through the use of indigenous aides who serve as intake workers. At termination, these workers also evaluate the services given by the center. A number of established agencies, such as state employment and public assistance, give services within the center in ways that are adapted to the needs and circumstances of this clientele. Hence, the service center constitutes a unitary social system in its own right while being made up of sub-systems, some of which are formalized and some of which are not, and which serve the population of a given geographic area.

Services given are not only tangible in terms of financial assistance, employment counseling, placement, legal services, etc., but long-range in terms of studying and documenting problems common to large sub-groups (e.g., the violation of civil rights in housing and courts of law), so that client groups can be mobilized in problem-solving efforts on a community scale. Within the context of the latter function, the indigenous person who works in intake may carry the role of worker within one context and the role of client in another context. Students placed in this setting have been able to move into this social system and its complex sub-systems with this frame of reference, which helps them define client and social systems, problems to be focused upon in a helping process, and differential processes employed to achieve specified goals. Currently, a third-year student in this placement is projecting an in-service training program for the hierarchy of employee roles encompassed in this system.

Another indication of integrated behavior, which is characteristic of the stage of generalization, is the impetus on the part of field instructors to make the field instruction sequence a balanced and unified entity in itself. I referred earlier to the efforts of field instructors to learn a new frame of reference from peers, and to develop new designs for courses. This activity continues and has its own set of issues and problems. Nonetheless, a core of field teachers has moved to the point where the central concern and interest lies in the integration of the field sequence as an independent unit. There has emerged a separate identity for the sequence, and a willingness to put what it has "on the line." Its current activities tap the special talents and know-how of the many teachers represented.

I have already mentioned the increasingly active role taken by students in pushing their goals. As a faculty, we think our curriculum has challenged and engaged students in thinking through some of their own broad objectives and demands. It has also provided us with a handle for active discussion and ongoing collaboration. Students have representation on our Curriculum Committee and on sequence committees which deal with curriculum development. Here students have the opportunity to see first hand how the curriculum evolves, the issues that emerge, and the progressive tasks that transform it into a program. Students come to understand better their role as consumers and reactors. They tend to make good suggestions, so that this level of interaction between students and faculty tends to be productive. There is nothing artificial or contrived about it. When a new segment of the curriculum is to be put into operation, many students already know the rationale for it and are able to interpret it to their peers. They are also able to help clarify questions and issues for which we have no immediate answers. By the same token, because flexibility and imagination have been required of field teachers in this curriculum, they are more comfortable in dealing with questions, challenges, and demands posed by students in relation to field courses. In a sense, all of us care about finding ways to meet the challenges and issues of our world of today, and enhanced communication along the whole network of the school's social system helps us to work on the issues rather than to expend our energies unproductively.

CONCLUSION

In conclusion, I would like to reiterate that we are living in a time of rapid change which calls for a willingness to be challenged by the issues of our profession, and a capacity to embark educationally on experimental and unconventional programs. This does not mean that we are casting aside what we know. It does mean that we are attempting to gain new perspectives about our assumptions, about what we know, and about what we do not know. This is particularly pertinent in our profession, where little practice theory has been validated. Impairment of social functioning in large segments of our society challenges us to seek new ways of effective problem-solving. Now more than ever, we need to build and validate theories to guide us in our tasks, and they must provide better methods for solving a range of enormously complicated problems and issues. True, what we are embarked upon continues to have elements of trial-and-error learning and doing. However, we have new knowledge perspectives to discipline our thinking and doing. In addition, we are forging tools, primitive as they may be, to analyze and evaluate what we are doing.

Within this context, retooling injects new ideas and ideals into the picture and is directed at forging new instruments for making them real and useful. This is an ongoing process punctuated by characteristic behavioral changes. It also makes manageable the demands for rapid change which are characteristic of our era.

SELECTED CSWE PUBLICATIONS
ON
FIELD INSTRUCTION

FIELD LEARNING AND TEACHING: EXPLORATIONS IN GRADUATE SOCIAL WORK EDUCATION. Proceedings of the Symposium Working Party on Field Learning and Teaching held in New Orleans in November, 1967. (#67-90-11) $3.00

FIELD INSTRUCTION IN GRADUATE SOCIAL WORK EDUCATION: OLD PROBLEMS AND NEW PROPOSALS. Articles by Sikkema, Regensburg, Dana. 1966. (#66-90-01) $3.00

AGENCY BOARD, EXECUTIVE, AND SUPERVISORY SUPPORT CONDUCIVE TO PRODUCTIVE FIELD INSTRUCTION. Workshop Report, APM, 1962. (#62-18-24) $1.00

EDUCATIONAL DEVELOPMENT IN SOCIAL GROUP WORK: AN EXAMINATION OF LEARNING OBJECTIVES, TEACHING METHODS, FIELD INSTRUCTION AND STUDENT PERFORMANCE. A group of papers, APM, 1962. (#62-18-26) $3.00

STUDY OF FIELD INSTRUCTION FOR INTERNATIONAL STUDENTS IN SCHOOLS OF SOCIAL WORK IN THE UNITED STATES AND CANADA. Prepared for the Committee on International Social Welfare Education. 1957. (#7-19-4) $1.00

THE EXPANSION OF CORRECTIONAL FIELD PLACEMENTS AND INTERNSHIPS. REPORT OF A MOUNTAIN STATES INSTITUTE, 1964. 1965. (#65-96-4) $3.00

POTENTIALS AND PROBLEMS IN THE CHANGING AGENCY-SCHOOL RELATIONSHIPS IN SOCIAL WORK EDUCATION, mimeographed. 1967. (#6-26-07) $1.00